Studies in Public Choice

Founding Editor

Gordon Tullock

Volume 41

Series Editor

Randall G. Holcombe, Florida State University, Tallahassee, FL, USA

The Studies in Public Choice series, inaugurated in 1979, is dedicated to publishing scholarship in the field of public choice and constitutional political economy. Springer and Series Editor, Randall G. Holcombe, welcome proposals for research monographs, edited volumes and reference works in all areas of public choice and constitutional political economy.

More information about this series at http://www.springer.com/series/6550

James T. Bennett

The History and Politics of Public Radio

A Comprehensive Analysis
of Taxpayer-Financed US Broadcasting

 Springer

James T. Bennett ⓘ
George Mason University
Fairfax, VA, USA

ISSN 0924-4700
Studies in Public Choice
ISBN 978-3-030-80021-5   ISBN 978-3-030-80019-2   (eBook)
https://doi.org/10.1007/978-3-030-80019-2

This Springer imprint is published by the registered company Springer Nature Switzerland AG
The registered company address is: Gewerbestrasse 11, 6330 Cham, Switzerland

Acknowledgements

I am especially grateful to my talented, long-time, and amazingly helpful editor, Bill Kauffman, for I am indebted to him for significant contributions to this study. I also thank Stuart A. Paul for his conscientious research assistance.

Contents

Contents

Chapter 1
Introduction

The Nielsen Company reported in late 2019 that 272 million Americans listen to "traditional radio" each week, more than the number who watch television, use a smartphone, or access the Internet.[1] For a medium whose death knell has been sounded, serially, at the advent of television, the Internet, and now podcasts, radio has proved remarkably indestructible.[2] Yet almost from the start, radio has also been excoriated as a noise box of inanity, a transmitter of low-brow entertainment, and, even worse, as an instrument of cultural degradation that promotes vapid popular music, and a medium whose ultimate purpose is merely to convince listeners to purchase the goods and services that are incessantly hawked by the advertisers who underwrite the programs and, it is alleged, effectively dictate content.

Concurrent with these critiques has been the existence of an alternative conception of radio as a vehicle for education, for uplift, for cultural and intellectual (and even political) enlightenment. Those articulating this perspective, largely based at first in colleges and universities, envisioned radio as a tool for education, not only in the schools but also in local communities as well. Most—though, significantly, not all—of them disdained advertising revenue and sought to have their vision subsidized by foundations, wealthy patrons, or various levels of government.

The long and winding road of educational radio would lead, eventually, to the creation of National Public Radio, which today insists on being known solely by the acronym NPR. A fixture on the left of the dial, NPR can be seen as either consummation or corruption of the vision of the educational radio movement. Prized by many liberals, especially affluent whites, and disparaged by many conservatives, especially those of a more libertarian bent, NPR has become a potent symbol of the political polarization and cultural chasm that characterizes the American conversation in these first decades of the twenty-first century.

The History and Politics of Public Radio: A Comprehensive Analysis of Taxpayer-Financed US Broadcasting examines the birth, growth, development, and maturation of educational radio—as well as the roads less traveled, the roads untraveled, the roads perhaps yet to be traveled.

© The Author(s), under exclusive license to Springer Nature Switzerland AG 2021
J. T. Bennett, *The History and Politics of Public Radio*, Studies in Public Choice 41,
https://doi.org/10.1007/978-3-030-80019-2_1

The exigencies and opportunities of wartime typically result in vast expansion of governmental power. This was particularly true of the U.S. during the First World War, and as Chap. 2 documents, the infant technology of radio was targeted by powerful government officials, led by the Secretary of the Navy, for nationalization. That campaign fell short, although in Europe, especially under the totalitarian regimes in Nazi Germany and the Soviet Union, centralized governments would employ radio as a principal means to spread propaganda.

In the early years of the New Deal, U.S. advocates of educational radio attempted to reserve a portion of the federally issued licenses for themselves. Though frustrated by a lack of support from the Roosevelt administration, they made a serious push for license reallocation, arguing that only noncommercial radio could meet the intellectual, cultural, scientific, and educational needs of the listening audience. This effort failed, though it may be seen as planting the seeds of later federal support of such stations.

The two decades following the conclusion of the Second World War were relatively quiescent in the field, though as Chap. 3 reveals, this was also an age in which new possibilities arose. The stodgy old university-dominated form of educational radio was waning, a victim of apathy, boredom, and the rise of television, but an energetic and voluntaristic alternative model was developed by anarchist-pacifist Lewis Hill, whose Pacifica Radio was evidence that a challenging, culturally avant-garde radio station (and later network) which was open to various expressed viewpoints could find an audience—and could also survive without (at first) government subvention.

Chapter 4 reviews the Carnegie Commission on Educational Television, a blue-ribbon establishmentarian panel whose 1967 report was the template for the Public Broadcasting Act of 1967. The Carnegie Commission's mixture of high-flown rhetoric and confident assertion of the necessity of federal support won the day over a disorganized and not terribly passionate opposition. Radio wasn't even an afterthought to the Carnegie commissioners, but savvy and determined activists, centered around the University of Michigan's campus radio station, achieved a landmark and rather surreptitious triumph with the late appending of the words "and radio" to wherever "television" appeared in the Johnson administration's draft legislation. They were aided by a hastily compiled study titled *The Hidden Medium: A Status Report on Educational Radio in the United States*, which had concluded that government subsidy was essential to the maintenance, if not flourishing, of the genre.

Chapter 5 elucidates the rapid divergence of theory and practice of the newborn National Public Radio. The early visionary of NPR, a Buffalo station manager named Bill Siemering, set out his hopes for the organization in its founding document, "National Public Radio Purposes." This was a youthful, optimistic, full-throated statement which foresaw the development of an open, welcoming, small-d democratic, and community-minded system of radio stations that would cover and also reflect their cities and regions in all their particularistic variety. A localist ethos was at the core of this vision, which was most emphatically not to be Washington-centric.

National Public Radio's earliest offerings, for instance *All Things Considered*, sometimes strove for such an effect, but soon NPR lost its mild counterculture, participatory democracy-flavored character and took on an establishment tone, becoming the radio counterpart of the *New York Times* and *Washington Post*. Politically, NPR made a powerful enemy in Richard Nixon, the first in a line of Republican presidents who have sought to reduce or even eliminate its budget. But it was a Carter appointee, veteran Democratic operative Frank Mankiewicz, who sought to wean the organization off federal funds—and under whose tenure NPR nearly went under.

Despite cursory and not very convincing denials by its defenders, National Public Radio has exhibited a measurable political bias since its founding. Its news coverage and its assumptions have been solidly within the liberal Democratic mainstream, and this tilt has drawn consistent fire from conservatives, libertarians, Republicans, and a number of leftists as well. Chapter 6 presents and assays these bias claims and examines the controversies over NPR's coverage of Bush 41 and Bill Clinton-era Supreme Court nominees.

Chapter 7 takes a closer look at the most serious and sustained effort to defund NPR: that of Speaker of the House Newt Gingrich and the Republican-controlled House of Representatives elected in November 1994. A central contention of the abolitionists was that NPR was "elitist," and both scholarly studies and NPR's own data reveal that its listeners do fit a demographic profile that contrasts sharply with that of non-listeners in terms of wealth, formal education, and residence. This chapter also recounts the scandals of the second decade of the twenty-first century which have given new energy to the organization's critics.

So, is NPR, having weathered political assaults for nearly half a century, eternal? Chapter 8, the conclusion, surveys a range of policy options from the left, the right, and the independent center. In the Social Media age of Sirius radio, online streaming, and a podcast in every earbud, even NPR's friends are proposing reformation, sometimes along the lines of those early apostles of educational radio. Meanwhile, those who view it as superfluous, didactic, or unconstitutional have renewed their efforts to end once and for all the federal subsidy of public radio.

And to think it all began with weather forecasts for farmers....

Notes of chapter

1. "Audio Today 2019: How America Listens," June 2019, https://www.nielsen.com/wp-content/uploads/sites/3/2019/06/audio-today-2019.pdf.
2. Podcast listenership is expected to exceed 160 million by 2024, marking an annual compound growth rate of 17 percent from 2014. Amy Watson, "Number of podcast listeners in the U.S. 2014–2023," *Statista*, December 9, 2019, https://www.statista.com/statistics/786826/podcast-listeners-in-the-us/.

Chapter 2
Don't Give the Public What It Wants;
Give the Public What It *Needs*

The wireless of Guglielmo Marconi, the young Italian inventor, enabled the transmission of signals over distances of several miles. At the dawn of the twentieth century, its applications seemed potentially limitless: military, trade, commercial, journalistic, or even just as a means of person-to-person communication. Within the first decade of the new century, the dots and dashes and beeps of Morse Code were joined by the first crackle of human voices, and the virgin airwaves would eventually begin to fill with gold (operatic performances) and dross (political speeches) alike. In time, Morse Code would give way to Rush Limbaugh, Vin Scully, and Wolfman Jack. Radio was here: for good…for ill…for enlightenment…or maybe for drilling state propaganda into the heads of the populace.

It was assumed by most that the new "wireless" technology would be "employed only for point-to-point communication."[1] The U.S. Navy utilized it to communicate between ships and shore; it was envisioned as a helpful maritime aid, broadcasting weather information and assisting rescues at sea, and helping distressed ships. The physicists and engineers who undertook research in the infant radio industry at the nation's universities envisioned it as a useful tool with which to impart weather and market reports to farmers. So, rather than point-to-point communication, they envisioned radio as a point-to-mass technology through which large audiences might be reached, even edified. As is typical with infant technologies, the later course of its development could barely be discerned. At the time, the eminently practical use of radio to offer advice on crop rotation passed for visionary.

Colleges and universities set up radio laboratories to test the applications of this new tool, though students being students, much of what was transmitted was "coded jargon, gibberish, and esoteric jokes of laboratory periods."[2] (It's good to know that some things never change.) As early as January 1914, however, the University of North Dakota was transmitting forecasts of the United States Weather Bureau to a nonuple of "nine amateur operators who then distributed the forecasts to farmers." Nebraska Wesleyan University, operating with the call letters 9YD, provided a similar service to Cornhuskers.[3]

© The Author(s), under exclusive license to Springer Nature Switzerland AG 2021
J. T. Bennett, *The History and Politics of Public Radio*, Studies in Public Choice 41,
https://doi.org/10.1007/978-3-030-80019-2_2

This being the Progressive Era, the government was not about to allow the new medium to develop without a guiding hand, especially since more than 1,000 amateur ham radio operators were fiddling around in their garages and makeshift laboratories, far from the oversight of officialdom. This was a bottom-up phenomenon, unregulated and, in its nerdish way, unruly. It needed regulation, or so the authorities believed. Complaints by the U.S. Navy of ham-sourced disruption provided an excellent pretext for federal action.

So the Radio Act of 1912 mandated licensing of radio transmitters and operators by the U.S. Secretary of Commerce and Labor. Educational institutions, particularly departments of physics, dominated the lists of early licensees, though the act set aside most of the electromagnetic spectrum for naval use. (About 1,000 licenses were issued.) Nevertheless, educational broadcasters can justly claim to be forerunners of their commercial brethren in the employment of radio as a mass medium. They were, as the history of communications scholar Robert W. McChesney says, "the true pioneers of U.S. broadcasting."[4]

World War I interrupted the parturition of radio as a means of civilian communication. The Wilson administration, which was effectively nationalizing industries (railroad, telephone, ocean shipping) and cracking down on freedom of speech and dissent (through its Espionage and Sedition Acts), set its sights on radio even before the U.S. entered the Great War. *Scientific American*, in its February 3, 1917, issue, which was dated less than ten weeks before Uncle Sam renounced his traditional neutrality with respect to European conflicts, editorialized against Secretary of the Navy Josephus Daniels's campaign to essentially abolish commercial uses of the wireless technology and place it under a Navy-directed government monopoly. (Among Secretary Daniels's underlings was a young New Yorker, Franklin D. Roosevelt, who served as Assistant Secretary of the Navy. The two would remain in touch on matters—including communications policy—into Roosevelt's presidency.)

The Navy, declared Secretary Daniels, "strongly recommends the Committee [on the Merchant Marine and Fisheries of the U.S. House of Representatives] provide for the purchase of *all* [emphasis added] stations used for commercial purposes" rather than coastal stations alone, as was envisioned by the legislation under consideration. He proposed that once these stations had been purchased for the Navy, no licenses would be subsequently issued by the federal government. The goal, as a critical *Scientific American* explained, "obviously" was "eventual Government ownership of all communication lines in the country."[5] The unrealized potential of the infant industry of radio as a means of communication among free people would be strangled in its cradle by the military.

Just a week later, *Literary Digest* surveyed what it called an impending "war" pitting the military against commercial and scientific interests over control of radio communications. It quoted John L. Hogan Jr., chief research engineer of National Electric Signaling Co., who warned, "The military interests of the Federal government, acting in the name of 'preparedness,' are now urging further and stricter laws to govern the commercial operation of radio-telegraphy….The outcome is not yet in sight, but the conflict promises to be memorable. Its result will determine whether radio-signaling in the United States will continue to hold its present position of preeminence, or whether the art will be subject to the initiative-killing, suppressive policies of military ownership and domination." (In those days before the emergence of what President Dwight Eisenhower would call the "military-industrial complex," Americans were less restrained in their strictures on the military.)

Sounding a similar note, the editor of *The Electrical World* cautioned that government ownership would extinguish the spirit of experimentation and enterprise in this aborning field: "American progress in radio-communication has been particularly rapid," he said, "because the art has not been a government monopoly here, but has been open to free competition from all parts of the country." Should the U.S. enter the war, it would be far better served by a radio industry that had developed freely, without the heavy regulatory hand of the military squelching the necessary spark of creativity.[6]

The federal government assumed control of this nascent technology on April 6, 1917, the day the United States declared war upon Germany—and it didn't want to let go. As Jesse Walker, author of *Rebels on the Air: An Alternative History of Radio in America*, writes, "Fifty-three commercial stations were taken over, along with the telegraph and telephone systems; the remainder were shut down. The production and distribution of radio components also came under naval direction, though private ownership was preserved."[7] In addition, over 6,000 amateurs were ordered to cease transmitting or receiving messages. The pretext was the allegation that German propagandists were listening in and exploiting wireless stations in New Jersey.[8]

Cooperation, even collaboration, was the surest path to survival. University of Wisconsin station WHA (née 9XM; it received its new call letters in 1922), among the most storied of broadcast pioneers, had been licensed to transmit in 1914 and began disseminating weather information in December 1916. It survived the Great War by sending out information to the Great Lakes Naval Training Station and the Navy radio station on Mackinac Island, among other nearby naval installations.[9] Institutions of higher learning such as St. Louis University and Tulane University trained radio operators for military service. (The first university to offer courses in non-military radio broadcasting was, perhaps fittingly, the University of Southern California.[10])

The coming-out party for propaganda as a major force in American life was made possible, or at least greatly aided, by U.S. intervention in the First World War. The administration of President Woodrow Wilson sold the war to a traditionally war-reluctant American public with an all-out propaganda blitz coordinated by the newly created U.S. Committee on Public Information (CPI), headed by journalist George Creel, a committed progressive who believed in propaganda as a noble pursuit akin to the "propagation of faith."[11] The CPI produced films, advertisements, pamphlets, and, most notoriously, enlisted 75,000 "Four-Minute Men" who were authorized to make brief speeches on behalf of the war effort at all manner of public gatherings, from movie theaters to town meetings. The CPI boasted that more than 7.5 million speeches were made under its auspices. George Creel denied that he was manufacturing propaganda. That was what the other side was doing. Rather, "Our effort was educational and informative throughout, for we had such confidence in our case as to feel that no other argument was needed than the simple, straightforward presentation of facts."[12]

Commercial radio, perhaps conceptualized but yet to be conceived, played no role in the World War I propaganda blitz, but that potential was grasped by the propagandists. Foremost among them was Edward Bernays, Sigmund Freud's double nephew and author of the classic volume *Propaganda* (1928).[13] Bernays got his start in the Committee on Public Information's Latin-American section. (Having developed his craft, Bernays, working on behalf of the United Fruit Company, would play a more central role in the 1954 U.S. overthrow of Guatemalan President Jacobo Árbenz.) Bernays cobbled together *Propaganda* from pieces he had published in, among other places, *Advertising and Selling* and *The American Journal of Sociology*: an eye-opening combo. His interests were both scholarly and practical; it was what we might call mindful propaganda. As Mark Crispin Miller writes, "Far from denoting lies, half-truths, selective history or any of the other tricks that we associate with 'propaganda' now, that word meant, at first, the total opposite of such deceptions."[14] Its earliest meaning was attached to the missionary work of the Catholic Church and signified the propagation, or dissemination, of doctrine and belief. There was no suggestion of hoodwinking the recipient of propaganda, of making her believe, *1984*-like, that we had always been at war with Oceania.

It was only in the First World War that the word took on its negative meaning of biased or invidious information used to promote a particular cause or point of view. Within a span of less than five years, propaganda had played a significant role in the deaths of millions of young men throughout Europe. Miller writes that this was "an extraordinary state accomplishment: mass enthusiasm at the prospect of a global brawl that otherwise would mystify those very masses, and that shattered most of those who actually took part."[15] The "Huns" and "Gerries" were said to be agents of barbarism, spearers of babies in their cribs, whereas the Anglo-American alliance was said to be fighting to make the world safe for democracy—which would have come as news to the natives of India and other British colonies, not to mention African-Americans who were being deprived of voting and other rights in the American South.

Edward Bernays, a self-declared "propagandist for propaganda," tried to "rid the word of its bad smell," writes Miller. He was no advocate of crude, bash-the-subject-over-his-head agit-prop. His propagandists would be "a benign elite of rational manipulators."[16] The ordinary American was too busy, too preoccupied with mundane matters, or maybe just too dull of mind to understand the complicated questions of modern life. So he or she would be guided by their intellectual superiors into the proper course of attitude and action.

Those at the top, or rather those in control of the instruments of power, had a responsibility to guide the rest of us toward the correct view of things, said Bernays. "The conscious and intelligent manipulation of the organized habits and opinions of the masses is an important element in democratic society," he wrote in *Propaganda*. The sheer size and complexity of modern society demanded that we be supervised by "a relatively small number of persons…who understand the mental processes and social patterns of the masses." They "pull the wires which control the public mind."[17]

Bernays was not lamenting this development. He was analyzing it, and approving of it, too, for he believed that without the guidance of manipulative propaganda, all would be chaos and confusion. It was "inevitable" in a democracy, he claimed, that a small number of influential people would "mold the mind of the masses that they will throw their newly gained strength in the desired direction."[18]

Propaganda was "the executive arm of the invisible government." Like any tool, it was neither good nor bad in itself, though it could be put to good or bad uses. Bernays regretted that the word had taken on sinister overtones. He preferred "public relations counsel" to "propaganda specialist" as the title for those who sought to mold the views of the public, whether promoting commercial products or political ideas.[19] Euphemism was, even at this early stage, an instrument in the bag of tricks. "Radio is at present one of the most important tools of the propagandist," noted Bernays, almost as an aside, adding only the unhelpful observation that "Its future development is uncertain."[20]

Walter Lippmann, the journalist and co-founding editor of *The New Republic* who had urged President Wilson to ramp up propaganda efforts to convince Americans of the necessity of U.S. intervention in the First World War, coined the term "manufacture of consent" to describe the process by which elites shape public opinion. Noam Chomsky, linguist and radical social critic, reframed the picture with his argument that the "prevailing conception" of the role of the media in a democratic society is one in which "the public must be barred from managing of their own affairs and the means of information must be kept narrowly and rigidly controlled."[21]

The implications of the manufacturing of consent were dire. Sociologist Paul Lazarsfeld wrote of the possible uses of radio by totalitarian governments: "If a government monopolizes the radio, then by mere repetition and by exclusion of conflicting points of view it can determine the opinions of the population."[22] Totalitarians instinctively understood this. So did more garden-variety authoritarians.

But there was pushback. There would always be pushback against those who sought to control the means of information.

Postwar, U.S. Secretary of the Navy Josephus Daniels urged a complete government takeover of radio. He told a congressional committee in December 1918 that "the passage of this bill will secure for all time to the Navy Department the control of radio in the United States," for "it is my profound conviction and is the conviction of every person I have talked with in this country and abroad who had studied this question that it must be a monopoly. It is up to the Congress to say whether it is a monopoly for the government or a monopoly for a company."[23] Secretary Daniels, not a man given to overpraising private initiatives or the unregulated activities of individuals, credited the Navy with the development of radio, "this near-miraculous communication." In his memoirs, published in the midst of the next world war, he said that "it would have been wise if [the growth of radio] had been continued under Navy direction in peace as well as war."[24]

As Erik Barnouw writes in his classic history *Tube of Plenty* (1990), Daniels and the government monopolists were met by a feisty opposition consisting of amateur radio enthusiasts and skeptics of monopoly. The American Radio Relay League emphasized that tens of thousands of American men had learned the art and practice of radio transmission in the recent war; were their skills to rust as they returned to private life? And Rep. William S. Greene (R-MA) declared, "I have never heard before that it was necessary for one person to own all the air in order to breathe... Having just won a fight against autocracy, we would start an autocratic movement with this bill."[25]

Within the naval department, at least from below decks, critics of Daniels surfaced. As Philip T. Rosen notes, Captain William H.G. Bullard, director of naval communications, and Commander Stanford C. Hooper, chief of the Radio Division of the Bureau of Engineering, urged the Navy to concentrate its radio efforts on the coasts and at sea and to leave the development of the nascent technology to private industry. After a year and a half of the unprecedented exercise of federal government powers over speech, the press, industry, and the economy, national "sentiment," said Commander Hooper, "is thoroughly against government ownership."[26]

Thus, in the less frenzied environment of peacetime, the Navy bill was sunk.

There was, as Philip T. Rosen writes in his history of the relationship between radio and the federal government in the interwar era, "nothing inevitable about the way American broadcasting turned out." Had the US Navy had its way, the medium, as a commercial or educational entity, would have come to naught, for the Naval Communications Service favored a ban on broadcasting "because it represented a frivolous use of the nation's airwaves."[27] But the naval offensive was repulsed, and the medium developed along parallel if related tracks: the commercial and the educational.

The first commercial station is often thought to be KDKA of Pittsburgh, whose 100-W station, licensed to Westinghouse in October 1919, broadcast to about 2,000 virgin listeners the results of the Harding-Cox "return to normalcy" election of November 2, 1920. The number of stations would climb exponentially, from just eight in 1920–21 to more than 500 in 1922 and over 700 in 1926.[28] (No distinction was made between licenses for commercial and educational stations.) The number of radio sets in use skyrocketed from 50,000 in early 1921 to 600,000 one year later.[29]

Dozens of colleges and universities, from land-grant giants like the universities of Wisconsin and Minnesota to faith-based schools such as the Latter-day Saints University of Salt Lake City (today's LDS Business College), received broadcast licenses in 1921–22. The far-sighted, or perhaps dreamiest, of the educational radio enthusiasts saw vast and wondrous potential within the medium. Historian George H. Gibson writes, "To bring their dreams to fruition, colleges broadcast from stadiums, auditoriums, and lecture halls. They offered sporting events for public relations and publicity, dramas and concerts for adult entertainment and education, and complete courses for college credit." Yet among the professoriate, "most damned radio with their indifference." It was seen as a novelty, unserious, unscholarly, even frivolous.[30]

Attendees at the First National Radio Conference in Washington, DC, in February 1922 heard Secretary of Commerce Herbert Hoover emphasize that education was to be a primary purpose of this incipient medium. By the fourth such conference, held in 1925 in the nation's capital, 129 educational institutions were broadcasting, though the sheer tedium of most of their output resulted in a rapid loss of market share, to use a later term, to the flashier commercial broadcasters.[31] Yet as a later promoter of the genre argued, educational radio "was not, as many believe, an afterthought, but the core of the country's earliest broadcasting operations."[32] It was a road potentially traveled.

Hoover, a skillful bureaucratic in-fighter and turf-expander, would struggle against the mundane Post Office and the blunderbuss Navy, mostly successfully, on behalf of his Commerce Department for dominion over the radio. He had no propagandistic ambitions, but the engineer in him abhorred disorganization. Hoover's bailiwick was challenged by a 1926 ruling of the US District Court for the Northern District of Illinois which denied the Secretary of Commerce the authority to dictate hours, wavelengths, and the power of stations, and found that "the selective issuance of broadcast licenses was unconstitutional."[33] In response, Congress enacted the Radio Act of 1927. The Radio Act required the acquisition of a license to operate a radio station, and created a five-member Federal Radio Commission (FRC) to regulate the domestic radio industry. The FRC was authorized to allocate channels and determine the hours of operation and power of each station, as well as, to a limited degree, regulate content. Licenses were to be apportioned with a *partis pris* toward applicants who would most effectively promote the "public interest, convenience and necessity," which attorneys Erwin G. Krasnow and Jack N. Goodman have dubbed the "vague but oft-repeated Holy Grail clause" of U.S. broadcast law.[34] There's not much that can't be fit under that definition. The Radio Act's advertised purpose was to reduce the allegedly chaotic scramble for spectrum space and the resultant interference. The new FRC also had the power to deny or revoke licenses. Its lifetime was mayfly brief: it existed year-by-year, renewed annually by Congress until supplanted in the Federal Communications Act of 1934.

At this early stage, the field was open; radio seemed to have any number of possible futures. Government ownership remained the dream of some, though they no longer wished to locate that ownership in the Department of the Navy. For instance, Grover A. Whalen, whose long and colorful career included prominent positions with Wanamaker's department store and various bureaucratic fiefdoms in the New York City government, most notably as Police Commissioner of the city, advocated government control of the medium based in a big-is-beautiful ethic. He recommended the creation of "strong stations" under municipal control whose growth would be ensured by "cutting out poorer and weaker stations which broadcast inferior programs."[35] It was Darwinism adapted for the airwaves.

The "exercise of control must be by the government," insisted Whalen, who knew whereof he spoke, for he had been the prime promoter of the creation of WNYC, New York City's municipally owned station, which began broadcasting in 1924. Writing in *The Nation* with the grim voice of enforced centralization, he excoriated "stations of little power broadcasting programs that are not worthwhile."[36] Whalen's determination to wipe out weaker private stations should not be surprising. During his abbreviated stint as Police Commissioner of New York City, he was "noted for strict enforcement of Prohibition laws." He summed up his general philosophy of law in the memorable aphorism: "There is plenty of law at the end of a nightstick."[37] Lacking a nightstick, a government edict would do.

Mockery of the inanity of commercial radio became a staple of 1920s and 1930s social criticism. Dr. Lee de Forest, the controversial inventor who called himself "the Father of Radio"—a very disputed paternity—decried "the crass commercialism, the etheric vandalism of the vulgar hucksters, agencies, advertisers."[38] (Etheric vandalism: de Forest could turn a phrase.) For good measure, he execrated the "sickening crooning by degenerate sax players"[39] The choleric wit H.L. Mencken complained in 1931 that upon scanning the radio dial all he could find was "a long series of imbecile speeches by fifth-rate politicians and agitators, and an equally long series of stupid musical programmes done by fifth-rates."[40]

It was a cacophony of idiocy, gruel for the ear, prolefeed for the mind—or so asserted various high-brow critics. Descending from Olympus, Robert Maynard Hutchins, the University of Chicago president who would shortly thereafter have the courage to actually abolish football at his once-football-mad institution, ventured to speak to the meeting of the National Advisory Council on Radio in Education (NACRE) in Chicago of October 8, 1934. President Hutchins, exhibiting the too-rare wisdom found in his profession to acknowledge what he does not know, began by admitting, "My qualifications for discussing the pretentious title ('Radio and Public Policy') assigned to me are so meager that I am afraid I must disregard it altogether." He further announced that "It is presumptuous for a layman who never made any money to discuss the problems of an industry and to attempt to prescribe for it." Of course, Hutchins being Hutchins, and thus being incapable of letting pass the opportunity for pontification, he discoursed at some length on the problems and potential of the medium—after the half-jocular admission that "I never consume an educational program if I can help it. My attitude toward such programs is the same as my attitude toward exercise. I believe in it for others."

Nevertheless, Hutchins advised his audience to accommodate the reasonable requests of those seeking to elevate discourse over the airwaves lest their failure to do so might open the door to state control and propaganda: "*I hazard the guess that unless broadcasting can be made more successful [in its educational function] it will find itself in immediate danger of more drastic regulation, of taxation, of competition with publicly-owned stations, and even of government ownership.*" This last possibility, especially, presents "a grave danger of the political abuses of radio."

So how to fend off such statist incursions? First, Hutchins recommended, the industry must cease its mistreatment of educational broadcasters. At present, he said, they are getting short shrift when it comes to prime hours, their programs are shifted willy-nilly and often without advance warning if something better presents itself for airing, censorship of non-mainstream ideas is at least implicit, there is little to no experimentation in presentation or subject matter, and financial support is "erratic" at best.[41] Commercial broadcasters, he concluded, must treat their educational partners or contributors with a modicum of respect and not view their airing of such offerings as tokens or tribute to ward off those who would socialize the airwaves.

He demurred, however, from what would later become a basic demand of the educational broadcasters. "I do not want for education any additional broadcasting facilities whatever," said Hutchins, touching on a sensitive topic on which educational broadcasters themselves were of several minds. "What would we do with them if we had them? Time and support are one thing; facilities are quite another." Rather, he wanted "*the stations and the chains to provide the facilities, the time, and some part of the support and leave us to do what we are supposed to know how to do and what we may sometimes learn how to do, namely, the educating.*" Refreshingly unwilling to importune or make imperious demands, Hutchins admits, "Is this fair? I do not know."[42] But the alternative may well have been the nationalization of radio, and that, he believed, would be no less than a disaster.

He was not unmindful of the widespread indifference of Americans to uplift. "[T]here is no use in broadcasting a program to which no one listens," he said, though allocating broadcast time only on the basis of popular appeal is self-defeating, for "*the radio cannot pretend to be an educational instrument...if the sole test of every program is the number of people gathered around the receiving sets.*" Such a standard would limit programming to "the most ephemeral topics" and moot the entire point of educational broadcasting.[43]

Contempt for what was seen as the lowest common denominator programming of commercial radio sometimes shaded over into contempt for private human action. A writer in *The Nation* doubted that "an obsolete, unplanned, traditionally exploiting capitalist economy can pull the radio out of [the] bag and make it function in the interest of human progress and civilization." The problem was that the "advertisers hold the whip hand" and the medium subserves their needs and demands. Rather than rejecting the concept of the whip hand, centralizing leftists of the age advocated its transfer to the federal government as part and parcel of the "technical and economic rationalization of the system."[44] If advertising were banned, and private ownership of stations were prohibited, and if the national government held the whip hand, as it were, the citizenry would be properly catechized in socialism, thus paving the way for a post-capitalist United States.

Jerome G. Kerwin, a political scientist at the University of Chicago, wrote in 1934 a pamphlet, *The Control of Radio*, the title of which implies that the medium must, or will, be "controlled," and the only question is who would do the controlling. He noted that "in most countries, radio was early recognized as a most important contribution to military science" and therefore was either "rigidly" supervised or "absolutely" controlled by the state. In the United States (as well as Uruguay, he added), it was left to become nothing more than a "popular toy."[45] Government control can go too far, Kerwin conceded, instancing the new Nazi regime in Germany, which viewed radio as an ideal instrument of propaganda. In the words of Eugen Hadamovksy, head of the radio division of the Nazi Ministry of Propaganda, radio will "create so broad a basis for National Socialism among the people that one day the entire nation will be drenched through and through with our philosophy."[46]

The Nazi regime placed radio at the center of its propaganda efforts. Joseph Goebbels, the Third Reich's Minister of Propaganda, portentously predicted that "What the press was to the nineteenth century, radio will be to the twentieth." The commercialism and frivolity of American radio, so scorned by intellectuals, was not what Goebbels had in mind. Rather, he said, "German radio under National Socialist auspices must become the clearest and most direct instrument for educating and restructuring the German nation." Hadamovsky insisted that under the direction of the Propaganda Ministry, the medium "must mold the character and will of the German nation and train a new political type."[47] To mold character as quickly and extensively as possible, Goebbels ordered the mass manufacture of the modestly priced *Volksempfanger*, or People's Set. These were produced in profusion beginning in May 1933. As a result of the widespread purchase of People's Sets, the number of radio receivers in Germany grew from 4.3 million in January 1933 to 8.2 million just a year later.[48]

Totalitarian regimes had been quick to fasten upon radio as "an instrument for the fashioning of the public mind." One non-Bolshevik American author conceded that "in Russia the soviet regime has made constant and effective use of this medium, not only to supply the rudiments of education for peasants hitherto brutishly ignorant but likewise to inculcate among them the fundamentals of communist propaganda."[49] Inculcating the tenets of the regime in brutish peasants would be a frequent goal, sometimes stated and sometimes not, of advocates of state-directed radio.

Even more enthusiastic—chillingly so—was James Rorty (father of the famed philosopher Richard Rorty), writing in *The Nation* in 1934, who practically exulted, "In Russia Stalin uses the radio to manufacture Stalinists, although it may well be claimed that as a result of the wiping out of private vested interests we find in Russia the nearest approximation to a genuinely creative and cultural use of the instrument."[50] The act of the "wiping out of private vested interests" filled the cemeteries of Russia, and thus Rorty's praise comes close to an obscenity, but even the "constant and effective" claim is an exaggeration, as historian Stephen Lovell of King's College London has found in his studies of the development and use of radio as an instrument of Bolshevik propaganda in the early Soviet Union.

The first transmission of the human voice over the airwaves in Russia came in February 1919; two years later, Muscovites first listened over public loudspeakers to a "spoken newspaper," which is to say information conveyed via radio. (Lenin called radio "a newspaper without paper and without distances."[51]) *Radioperedacha*, a not entirely state-controlled radio company, began broadcasting regularly in late 1924 (and was obliterated in 1928, as non-state communications organs were inconsistent with Bolshevik ideology). The great Bolshevik hope of radio was that it enabled "the almost instantaneous dissemination of politicized information over huge distances," as Lovell writes. But that hope "fell some way" shy of the practice.[52]

As in the United States, the rise of radio in Russia was greatly aided by private operators, or radio hams, as they were called: often science-oriented male loners with pronounced individualistic streaks that made them poor material for the New Soviet Man. The Russian hams, who traded ideas in their periodical *Radioliubitel*, made their own receivers, their DIY spirit a rebuke to the collectivist ethos that the Bolsheviks sought to inculcate. Though largely proletarian in origin, they evinced little interest in furthering the dictatorship of the proletariat, and as Lovell notes, "[t]heir most treasured achievement was to pick up signals from America."[53] Nevertheless, the state tolerated them—at first.

Mass production of radio lagged in the Soviet Union, and as a result, individual ownership was rare in the 1920s, when ideological fervor was high and radio "formed the auditory component of the campaign against old peasant ways." This gave rise to an iconic image of early Soviet life: Russians gathered around loudspeakers at mass listening points—streetcorners, town squares, reading rooms, rural centers—taking in not only propaganda but music, theater, and other offerings. As late as 1939, notes Lovell, "more than 80% of radios (or 5.5 million) in the USSR were wired loudspeaker points."[54] While this may bear a surface resemblance to the hope of American enthusiasts that radio might serve as a kind of town meeting of the air, "splendidly sprawling bulletin boards," the communication went just one way: from the authorities to their subjects.[55] It was a case of We Talk—You Listen.

The primary propaganda purposes of Soviet radio were twofold: 1) antireligious; and 2) to upend peasant folkways and beliefs. Yet technological challenges meant that listenership was concentrated in cities, a "mismatch" of audience and message that Lovell calls the "uncomfortable paradox" of early Soviet radio. (Acknowledging the vast differences between the 1920s Soviet Union and the contemporary United States, a glaring mismatch can also be said to exist between NPR's audience—upper-middle-class, urban and suburban, politically liberal—and its message, if indeed proselytization is its purpose. If it means simply to preach to the converted, then the match is perfect.)

The effectiveness of Bolshevik anti-religious radio propaganda is questionable, and one reason, oddly, is that Soviet cultural offerings were too highbrow. Analyses have found that the music broadcast was overwhelmingly from the classical canon—Rimski-Korsakov, Tchaikovsky, Schubert, Beethoven, Grieg, and Mozart.[56] Yet the peasants who needed to be disabused of their religious beliefs preferred comedy and popular entertainment. (Again, there are parallels with NPR, though one hesitates to draw them.)

Listenability was also a problem. Stephen Lovell writes that most of the early broadcasters over Soviet radio were actors, many trained at the Moscow Arts Theatre; they were instructed to purge their accents of regional or provincial touches (rather as U.S. newsreaders on national sites have long done). They were also to avoid "bourgeois" or "aristocratic" styles of speech, and if a certain stiltedness crept into their readings who could blame them?[57] Slips of the tongue could result in firing at best, punishment as a treasonous counterrevolutionary at worst.

American boosters of government-directed or sponsored radio preferred the examples of Great Britain and Canada, whose BBC and CBC, respectively, were public corporations supported by fees on receiving sets. The BBC, Jerome Kerwin noted approvingly, aimed at raising "the general cultural level of the population; it is not to give the people what they want." What they emphatically did not want, he seems to admit, was to be educated or uplifted; they want, instead, low-brow entertainment. But in Kerwin's utopia, they would not get such. For "If education is to be the aim of radio broadcasting, it is absurd to talk at the same time, as some Americans do, of giving the public what it wants."[58] The public should get what it *needs*, and in this, it must be guided by their betters.

Kerwin's assumption that those who control the levers of power are more cultured or in possession of superior taste would not seem to have been borne out by a casual inspection of the American political scene of the 1930s. Even in New York City, a putative epicenter of high culture in the New World, Depression-era Mayor Fiorello

La Guardia was praising the management for the format of WNYC, which was owned by the city of New York. The Mayor declared: "Maestro, we're gonna keep that damn old radio station, and you're on the right track with that good music. Leave jazz to the other stations. I don't want any hot stuff." The lesson, as law professor Oscar G. Chase has noted, is that "government control follows its funds." The WNYC station manager, having received his marching orders from his funder, was not about to cross the mayor by plugging Duke Ellington into his lineup.[59]

Kerwin was most decidedly not amused by Radio Corporation of America (RCA) dynamo David Sarnoff's lecture: "What the public demands of radio is entertainment. If the educators on the air fail to recognize that fact in the development of education by radio, they are merely firing a blank cartridge. Every person entrusted with teaching by radio should be required to pass an examination on his ability as a showman. When education joins hands with radio, it enters the show business."[60]

Worried about the deleterious consequences of "the free play of private enterprise in industry and commerce," as well as the possibility that the "theory of rugged individualism will raise its hoary head," Jerome Kerwin counseled a preemptive strike on behalf of uplift and state control.[61] He urged the federal government to "erect its own chain of stations" on which advertising is forbidden and edifying educational programs are aired. As for its financing, he called upon his fellow citizens to "frankly face the necessity of governmental support from the public treasury." He would, however, permit the continued operation of some private stations, properly regulated, and "pending the establishment of central control of all communications."[62]

The United States was not Great Britain; the state would not enjoy a monopoly in this communications technology. But this was not to say that government would have no role whatsoever in radio. Perhaps, some suggested, it could reserve channels for nonprofit or educational institutions.

Interest groups arose and contended for influence, as will happen when government or foundation grants are available, or at least rumored to be in the offing. The group which Robert Maynard Hutchins addressed, the National Advisory Council on Radio in Education (NACRE), had been established in 1930 with funding from the Rockefeller Foundation and the Carnegie Corporation. It was not to be confused with the National Committee on Education by Radio (NCER), also created in 1930 and seeded with a five-year, $200,000 grant from the Payne Fund, most famous, or infamous, for subsidizing studies of the effects of movies on children, research that led to industry self-censorship via the Hays Code. The NCER in 1931 complained that commercial interests were transforming radio from a medium bursting with the promise of education and uplift into "the dollar sign's mightiest megaphone."[63]

Jesse Walker has characterized both NACRE and NCER as elitist uplifters whose "basic concern was that listeners were not getting enough spinach, and their basic demand was for government-guaranteed, educrat-run channels for the public's betterment."[64] (For their part, the new commercial radio networks that were coming under intense criticism protested that among their popular offerings were several programs of an educational nature. Their case was not strengthened, however, by NBC's inclusion of "Amos 'n Andy" in its list of putatively educational shows.[65])

Going these organizations several steps further was the National Congress of Parents and Teachers, forerunner of the famed Parent-Teacher Association (PTA), which in 1932 demanded "the complete nationalization and decommercialization of broadcasting." Yes, the proto-PTA weighed in firmly on the socialist side of the question. At this unusual historical moment, when socialist and even communist policies and parties were achieving the pinnacle of their influence in American political life, many newspapers and their unions also chimed in on the nationalizing side of the debate, in large part because they feared radio as a formidable competitor for scarce advertising revenue.[66]

Robert McChesney itemizes the critique of the radio status quo, circa 1930, as:

1. The airwaves are a public resource and should be treated as a public utility. Private ownership is an offense against the public.
2. Dependence on commercial interests would mean that radio would censor or ignore non-mainstream opinions.
3. The commercial system, by catering to the lowest common denominator, would tend to depress the cultural level of Americans.[67]

Still, calls for total nationalization were rare. Most envisioned a dual system in which commercial broadcasters shared the airwaves with educational broadcasters, who would be guaranteed a slice of the frequency pie and perhaps have their facilities, often threadbare, upgraded by the infusion of revenue from a tax on radio sets. Some proposed that these educational broadcasters operate under a quasi-governmental structure like the BBC, though the American Civil Liberties Union and those of a libertarian bent worried that this might create a state-sponsored propaganda network.[68]

A 1931 legislative offering by Senator Simeon Fess (R-OH) would have reserved 15% of radio frequencies for use by educational broadcasters. It was supported by the NCER but not by its near-acronymical soundalike NACRE, which preferred a cooperative approach under which "commercial stations…would give air time to programs produced by educational institutions."[69] In its moderation, NACRE was regarded as cringing collaborationists by some, practical realists by others. In any event, the Fess measure failed, though it set the stage for a contentious battle three years later. The battle, or perhaps scuffle is the more accurate noun since the apple cart never really came close to being upset, nevertheless would be considered, in retrospect, a climacteric moment in the history of federal radio policy.

The administration of President Franklin D. Roosevelt created a communications committee whose members included Commerce Secretary Daniel C. Roper, Senator Clarence Dill (D-WA), Representative Sam Rayburn (D-TX), Dr. Irwin Stewart of the Department of State, Dr. Walter M.W. Splawn of the Interstate Commerce Commission, and Major-General Charles Saltzman, then with the New York Telephone Company. Their task was to formulate a federal communications bill to centralize control of these new technologies in one administrative body.

The resultant Communications Act of 1934 begat the Federal Communications Commission, or FCC, the successor to the Federal Radio Commission. The seven-member (it was reduced to five in 1982) FCC "maintained essentially the same objectives as the Federal Radio Commission," as First Amendment scholar Jonathan W. Emord writes, though it broadened the federal government's oversight of content.[70] The airwaves were assumed to be owned by the public, which is to say the government; private interests were licensed to use specified frequencies but did not "own" them.[71] For our purposes, however, the salient feature, or nonfeature, of the Communications Act of 1934 was an unsuccessful amendment thereto—an amendment that the Roosevelt administration did nothing to advance, to the keen disappointment of those who believed that the moment for decisive action had come.

During FDR's first term, a government-run system was not entirely off the table in terms of national discussion. Josephus Daniels, the Navy Secretary who had urged the subordination of radio to military control under President Wilson, told his old subaltern in the Department of the Navy, Franklin D. Roosevelt, "I understand that a movement is on foot in Washington to make a monopoly of all communications—telegraph, telephone, radio, and cable. I am in favor of this if the monopoly is owned and controlled by the government, but strongly opposed to it if it is to be privately owned and operated. In the time of war, we must take over communications. The government should own and control them all the time. There is no more reason why other communications industries should be privately owned than the mails."[72] The implication here is that any means of communication not under the oversight of a benevolent central state ought to be barred, as was competition to the postal service.

Josephus Daniels did not succeed in his quest to secure a monopoly on radio by the national government, but in the early years of President Roosevelt's New Deal, the range of policy options did expand in reaction to the exigencies of the Great Depression. Partly in response to widespread complaints about the ubiquitous commercials on radio, Senators Robert Wagner (D-NY) and Henry Hatfield (R-WV) proposed an amendment to the Communications Act of 1934 requiring that one-quarter of all radio licenses be given to nonprofits. This was a successor, with the ante raised, to Senator Fess's 1931 proposal that 15% of radio channels be devoted to educational stations.

The issue had not lain dormant for the three intervening years. Groups such as the Federal Council of Churches and the American Bar Association had called for varying percentages of radio channels to be set aside for non-commercial broadcasters. But the movement's John the Baptist was Reverend John B. Harney, a Paulist father whose order operated a station with call sign WLWL. Father Harney, superior general of the 93 members of the Missionary Society of St. Paul the Apostle in the New York City region, had since 1925 overseen the development and struggles of WLWL, which in less than a decade had seen its airtime chopped from unlimited to two hours per day, as the CBS affiliate in Atlantic City, New Jersey, WPG, had nearly crowded the fathers out, with the assistance of the Federal Radio Commission. Founded in 1858, the Paulists had long used the media and the arts to propagate the faith, so the station was not all sermons and prayers. According to the Federal Radio Commission, WLWL devoted just 19% of its broadcast time to religious programs, with the majority classified as "entertainment" (51%) and another 10% "education."[73]

Father Harney testified before Senator Dill's Committee on Interstate Commerce on March 15, 1934, a sore thumb (or rose, depending upon one's view) in a lineup of witnesses that included David Sarnoff, president of the Radio Corporation of America. Father Harney staked out a position of radical reform or redistribution. He urged that the Federal Radio Commission revoke all licenses 90 days from the enactment of the law and reallocate them, with at least one-quarter of these licenses reserved for educational and nonprofit operators.[74] Well, that certainly got the attention of current radio licensees!

The relevant portions of Wagner-Hatfield read as follows:

"To eliminate monopoly and to insure equality of opportunity and consideration for educational, religious, agricultural, labor, cooperative, and similar non-profit-making associations, seeking the opportunity of adding to the cultural and scientific knowledge of those who listen in on radio broadcasts, all existing radio broadcasting licenses issued by the Federal Radio Commission…are declared null and void 90 days following the effective date of this act.…

The Commission shall reserve and allocate only to educational, religious, agricultural, labor, cooperative, and similar non-profit-making associations one-fourth of all radio broadcasting facilities.…[These] facilities…shall be equally as desirable as those assigned to profitmaking persons, firms, or corporations.…[T]he licensee may sell part of the allotted time as will make the station self-supporting." [By *facilities* the sponsors meant frequencies, power, and hours of operation.][75]

Father Harney emphasized that his was not a sectarian measure; it would benefit, he said, all faiths and denominations, as well as organizations promoting labor, agricultural, and cultural causes. Curiously, one potential ally, the Federal Council of Churches, did not endorse Harney's amendment, holding out for a 33% set-aside.[76] One wonders to what extent anti-Catholic sentiment motivated the overwhelmingly Protestant Council.

Representing the National Association of Broadcasters (NAB) at the hearings, Henry Bellows of CBS warned that a reallocation of licenses might "shut out" certain faiths (he mentioned Methodists, Jews, and Christian Scientists), who would find their rivals disinclined to give them airtime.[77] (Senator Dill drove home this point in a colloquy with Senator Marvel Logan (D-KY). Dill asked how the Congress or the appropriate regulatory agency would determine how many stations and how much airtime to give to Catholics, Protestants, and Jews, to which Senator Logan appended, "And to the Hindus." And don't forget the infidels, added Dill, after which Logan predicted that a "national association of atheists…would want some time."[78] One is surprised that they didn't mention Satanists as well!)

While Father Harney urged Senator Dill's committee to provide a set-aside for nonprofits in the Communications Act of 1934, Senator Dill urged Father Harney to settle for a thorough study of the matter. Dill explained that the NAB had offered nonprofits airtime for educational purposes, and wasn't that enough? Besides, how would these impecunious educators pay the operating expenses incurred by their allotted broadcast channels?

Under questioning from Senator James Couzens (R-MI), Father Harney said, "These licensees should have the right to sell some of their time so as to obtain enough to live on; not to make a profit, but enough to support themselves, so they will not be dependent on charity all the while and will not have to be beggars."[79] For what good would it do to gain one of these set-aside educational licenses if one was unable to muster the necessary operating funds? And how, absent an individual or foundational sugar daddy or a broad base of membership, would one amass these funds if not by selling advertising?

The Paulists were already doing so. And although they raised only about $3,000 annually from advertising, it wasn't from lack of trying. Nevertheless, Senator Dill charged, in floor debate, that Harney and his allies, though they "call themselves educational, religious, nonprofit stations," in fact were "planning to enter the commercial field and sell a tremendous amount of their time for commercial purposes."[80] This was almost certainly untrue, though Dill was on firmer ground in asserting that many of those stations lacked the facilities to be anything more than two-hour-a-day, low-power broadcasters.

The Harney amendment, as it was often called, failed in committee, but Senators Wagner and Hatfield pressed forward with a modified version on the Senate floor, aided by the substantial public-relations talents of Father Harney and other Catholic groups. Evidence of support included petitions in favor of Wagner-Hatfield bearing more than 60,000 signatures under the imprimatur of the Knights of Columbus, the Ancient Order of Hibernians, the National Council of Catholic Women, and other social and religious organizations of Catholics.[81] Harney's primary allies within the industry were the labor activists of WCFL, the voice of the Chicago Federation of Labor. As Robert McChesney details in his monograph on the WCFL, the American Federation of Labor (AFL), with which the Chicago Federation was affiliated, exhibited a distinct lack of interest in, or even mild support of, the station, preferring labor to buy time on commercial stations rather than run its own.

WCFL went on the air in 1926 in order to offer a "working-class perspective" on the issues of the day.[82] The Dubuque, Iowa-born electrician Edward N. Nockels, secretary of the CFL, spearheaded the radio effort.[83] Like Father Harney's WLWL, the station limited the amount of hortatory message-delivering over its airwaves, subordinating preaching and teaching, or didacticism, to such entertainment as "classical music, vaudeville and musical comedy, and dance music," as well as live reports from the Chicago Cubs and Chicago White Sox baseball games.[84]

Strikingly, both WLWL and WCFL solicited advertising, despite the disapproval of some educational radio theorists, but then the priests and union men who ran the stations existed in a real world in which bills must be paid. Lobbies and pressure groups were free to spin fantasies in which broadcasters who sought to elevate the public taste or inform the public mind received manna from heaven, or at least subsidies from Capitol Hill, but the people on the ground, or in the air, as it were— the people who actually broadcast these programs—understood that raising revenue from private sources, especially a broad base of private sources, was important not only to paying the bills but also maintaining independence from the government and state authorities.

And so the Chicago Federation of Labor's station, WCFL, endeavored to support itself by annual donations of one dollar per CFL member, by listener contributions, by nearly 100,000 subscriptions to the *WCFL Radio Magazine*, and, after it became apparent that these methods alone would not provide sufficient revenue, by selling advertising: a scrupulously libertarian approach.[85] Advertisers ranged from the Ford Motor Company to a patent medicine outfit going by the cheesy name of the Restoro Health Institute.[86]

Wagner-Hatfield galvanized the industry in opposition. *Variety* stated that "the NAB were in a panic checking off names of Senators and trying to pull wires and get votes."[87] Though the issue was usually relegated to the back pages of the nation's dailies, if it was mentioned at all, Henry A. Bellows of CBS told the National Association of Broadcasters that Wagner-Hatfield "obviously would have destroyed the whole structure of broadcasting in America."[88] Wagner-Hatfield was defeated on the floor of the U.S. Senate by a vote of 42–23, and though the proposal was introduced in the U.S. House of Representatives by Rep. Stephen Rudd (D-NY), it never reached the House floor, in part due to the firm opposition of Rep. Sam Rayburn, chairman of the House Committee on Interstate and Foreign Commerce.

While Edward Nockels of WCFL estimated that three-quarters of Congress supported a set-aside, Robert McChesney lays the defeat of the proposal primarily at the feet of the congressional committee chairmen, including Senator Dill of the Interstate Commerce Committee, whose opposition was critical in that era of powerful committee chieftains. Moreover, President Roosevelt stayed above the fray, which seemed perhaps a sideshow to the more important debates over elements of his economic New Deal.[89]

This was the great fork in the road, argues McChesney. "Roosevelt alone," he says, had the chance "to arrest the private and commercial domination of the American airwaves." By not acting, he consigned public ownership of the airwaves, and to an extent the potential of nonprofit educational stations, to a place beyond the fringe.[90] In this instance, at least, FDR acted to defend private enterprise, albeit a private enterprise that depended on federal licensing.[91]

As a sop to the Wagner-Hatfield forces, and a method of winning over fence-sitters, Senator Dill and the authors of the Communications Act of 1934 added Sect. 307(c), which authorized the FCC to study the question raised by the amendment and report to Congress forthwith, or by February 1, 1935. The National Committee on Education by Radio had been pushing for such a study, confident, as those with tunnel vision often are, that dispassionate researchers, as those on the government payroll were believed to be, would of course come to conclusions consonant with enlightened opinion, i.e., the opinion held by the NCER. To study a reallocation of licenses would be to endorse a reallocation of licenses.

Taking no chances, commercial broadcasters dominated the hearings, and "most of the testimony presented before the Commission was negative." Nor were educational broadcasters marching in lockstep, as some believed that they were already stretched to their capacity and would be unable to take on additional hours or afford the necessary equipment.[92] Father Harney, knowing when a fix was in, forbore from testimony, though as McChesney writes, he did show up unscheduled "to refute a vitriolic anti-Catholic and anti-Harney diatribe" by a Jehovah's Witness witness.[93]

Staking out the statist flank during the hearings was Dr. Floyd W. Reeves, personnel director of the Tennessee Valley Authority (TVA). Dr. Reeves presented a five-point program for radio:

1. Government would own and operate a national system of radio stations.
2. These would be placed at frequencies that would cause "as little disruption" of commercial facilities as possible.
3. Government would finance the network's operation.
4. The President would appoint a committee consisting of representatives of the "foremost non-profit national educational and cultural agencies" which would determine programming.
5. The national radio network's facilities would be available to government agencies and non-profits for the production and transmission of "educational and cultural programs."

Dr. Reeves's vision is not wholly incongruent with the eventual shape of National Public Radio, but even in 1934, when government direction or even ownership of industry was being debated seriously, his testimony was considered beyond the pale by the Roosevelt administration. The chairman of the TVA's board of directors, Arthur E. Morgan, quickly dashed off a telegram to the Federal Communications Commission setting the record straight and containing an implied rebuke of Reeves: "The Tennessee Valley Authority has not urged or favored governmental administration of radio stations. It is the opinion of the board of directors that the educational and cultural agencies of the country should have a reasonable use of the radio facilities of the country but that all such programs should be under non-governmental and non-partisan control and direction."[94] The TVA, a frequent target of conservatives and anti-socialists of the era, could not afford to go banging about in other fields, stirring up trouble. It had enough trouble of its own.

As it happens, TVA Chairman Morgan laid out his own ideas on "Radio as a Cultural Agency in Sparsely Settled Regions and Remote Areas" in a May 1934 speech in Washington, DC, to the National Committee on Education by Radio. Morgan was a civil engineer by training but a utopian—or dystopian, depending upon one's point of view—by disposition. President of the progressive Antioch College in his native Ohio, Morgan was an acolyte of the philosophy of Edward Bellamy, author of *Looking Backward*, the 1888 novel which imagined a collectivist future in which people labored for an "industrial army" and large institutions and technologies replaced smaller human-scale institutions. Like Bellamy, Morgan believed that a coercive central power could elevate and edify the common man, whose tastes would be raised beyond the plebian or demotic under the tutelage of his betters.

Thus, Morgan began his address to the NCER by contrasting the highbrow musical environment of educated Europe, where "people of exceptional taste, of exceptional discrimination," set the tone, with peasant Europe, whose "country fairs" were dominated by "the crudest of American jazz."[95] (This is a consistent theme among early advocates of educational radio: they absolutely *hated* jazz.) Left to their own devices and their own preferences, Morgan argued, the lower classes will choose lower forms of music and culture. Rural people, especially, are saddled with "an unrecognized sense of inferiority." They are largely incapable of creating their own cultural artifacts and will simply consume, without discrimination, whatever offerings are transmitted to them by the city. This is where radio comes in. The American peasantry will accept whatever comes over the airwaves as "coming from superior authority." So why not broadcast programs of merit, of refinement, of uplift? He was not a regular radio listener, Morgan told his audience of educational radio advocates. He had listened for an hour—one whole hour!—in preparation for his speech and found "scarcely anything that was great, scarcely anything that was the work of a master. Nearly all was trivial and very much of it debasing." Commercial interests had squandered an opportunity to enlighten their vast listenership. Their time was up.

Radio was at a crossroads. The old passé world of "rugged individualism" was being supplanted by "social planning" for the benefit of all.[96] Mass communications could spur this evolution along, not, Morgan emphasized, direct government control or ownership. That would carry with it "the danger of government propaganda." Rather, radio ought to develop along lines similar to that of private colleges and universities, with private funding sources, ample endowments, and direction from "well-known educators" and "public-spirited men."[97] Exactly how funds were to be procured for this endeavor he left for others to figure out.

Neither the Morgan nor the Reeves contending views within the TVA were reflected in the Federal Communications Commission's January 1935 report. The FCC punted on the proposal that Congress set aside a fixed percentage of radio facilities for non-profits, as had been expected, though it did so "respectfully," concluding that "at this time no fixed percentages of radio broadcast facilities be allocated by statute" to nonprofits.[98] While declining to recommend any such measure resembling Wagner-Hatfield, it did encourage nonprofits to make use of the superior facilities of commercial stations. It also urged a national conference which might bring together the best minds of the commercial and nonprofit radio world to elevate the medium and "better serve the public interest."[99] The conference was held just four months later, in mid-May 1935, and engendered a Federal Radio Education Commission, chaired by Dr. John W. Studebaker, U.S. Commissioner of Education.

As for Father Harney's WLWL, it limped along for two more years before the Paulists sold it to the Bulova watch company in 1937. The station took the new call letters WBIL. If Father Harney's crusade faltered, the gist of his proposal reappeared when in later years portions of the FM band were reserved for educational broadcasters, although the character of those organizations he had imagined dominating the nonprofit quarter of the dial—religious, labor, agricultural, cooperative—bears little if any resemblance to the content of today's NPR broadcasts.

Notes of Chapter

1.   Jesse Walker, *Rebels on the Air: An Alternative History of Radio in America* (New York: New York University Press, 2001), p. 13.
2.   George H. Gibson, *Public Broadcasting: The Role of the Federal Government, 1912–1976* (New York: Praeger, 1977), p. 1.

3.   J. Wayne Rinks, "Higher Education in Radio, 1922–1934," *Journal of Radio Studies*, Vol. 9, No. 2 (2002): 305. See also Werner J. Severin, "Commercial v. Non-Commercial Radio During Broadcasting's Early Years," *Journal of Broadcasting*, Vol. 22, No. 4 (Fall 1978): 491–92.
4.   Robert W. McChesney, "The Battle for the U.S. Airwaves, 1928–1935," *Journal of Communication* 40, No. 4 (Autumn 1990): 30.
5.   "Is Government Ownership of Wireless Intended?" *Scientific American*, February 3, 1917: 116.
6.   "Government Control of Wireless," *Literary Digest*, February 10, 1917.
7.   Walker, *Rebels on the Air: An Alternative History of Radio in America*, p. 26.
8.   Josephus Daniels, *The Wilson Era: Years of Peace—1910–1917* (Chapel Hill: University of North Carolina Press, 1944), p. 496.
9.   Severin, "Commercial v. Non-Commercial Radio During Broadcasting's Early Years," *Journal of Broadcasting*: 493.
10.   Rinks, "Higher Education in Radio, 1922–1934," *Journal of Radio Studies*: 306.
11.   Robert Jackall and Janice M. Hirota, *Image Makers: Advertising, Public Relations, and the Ethos of Advocacy* (Chicago: University of Chicago Press, 2000) p. 13.
12.   Mark Crisipin Miller, introduction to Edward Bernays, *Propaganda* (New York: Ig Publishing, 2005/1928), p. 14. See also Edward Bernays, *Crystallizing Public Opinion* (New York: Ig Publishing, 2011/1923).
13.   Bernays was the double nephew of Sigmund Freud, as Freud's sister was Bernays's mother and Freud's wife's brother was his father.
14.   Miller, introduction to Edward Bernays, *Propaganda*, p. 9.
15.   Ibid., p. 11.
16.   Ibid., pp. 15–16.
17.   Bernays, *Propaganda*, pp. 37–38.
18.   Ibid., p. 47.
19.   Ibid., pp. 48, 63.
20.   Ibid., p. 164.
21.   Noam Chomsky, *Media Control: The Spectacular Achievements of Propaganda*, Second Edition (New York: Seven Stories Press, 2002), p. 10.
22.   Quoted in Marshall McLuhan, *Understanding Media: The Extensions of Man* (Cambridge, MA: MIT Press, 1994/1964), p. 297.
23.   Erik Barnouw, *Tube of Plenty: The Evolution of American Television*, Second Revised Edition (New York: Oxford University Press, 1990/1976), p. 20.
24.   Daniels, *The Wilson Era: Years of Peace—1910–1917*, p. 496.
25.   Barnouw, *Tube of Plenty: The Evolution of American Television*, p. 21.
26.   Philip T. Rosen, *The Modern Stentors: Radio Broadcasters and the Federal Government, 1920–1934* (Westport, CT: Greenwood Press, 1980), p. 24.
27.   Ibid., pp. 3–4.
28.   Ibid., p. 7.
29.   Jerome G. Kerwin, *The Control of Radio* (Chicago: University of Chicago Press, 1934), p. 6.

30. Gibson, *Public Broadcasting: The Role of the Federal Government, 1912–1976*, pp. 3–4.
31. Ibid., p. 6.
32. Jerrold Sandler, "Educational Radio: The Broad Perspective," in *The Hidden Medium: A Status Report on Educational Radio in the United States* (New York: Herman W. Land Associates, April 1967), p. i.
33. Robert W. McChesney, "Franklin Roosevelt, His Administration, and the Communications Act of 1934," *American Journalism* V, No. 4 (1988): 206; "*United States v. Zenith Radio Corporation* et al.," 12 F 2nd (1926).
34. Erwin G. Krasnow and Jack N. Goodman, "The 'Public Interest' Standard: The Search for the Holy Grail," *Federal Communications Law Journal*, Vol. 50, Issue 3 (1998): 606. For an analysis of the FRC's actions with regard to content, see Jonathan W. Emord, *Freedom, Technology, and the First Amendment* (San Francisco: Pacific Research Institute, 1991), pp. 175–83.
35. Grover A. Whalen, "Radio Control," *The Nation*, Vol. 119, No. 3081 (July 23, 1924): 90.
36. Ibid., 90–91.
37. "Mr. New York: Grover Whalen's Unique Diplomacy," https://www.wnyc.org/story/216001-grover-whalen/, accessed August 20, 2019.
38. Rosen, *The Modern Stentors: Radio Broadcasters and the Federal Government, 1920–1934*, p. 164.
39. Kerwin, *The Control of Radio*, p. 23.
40. Rosen, *The Modern Stentors: Radio Broadcasters and the Federal Government, 1920–1934*, p. 8.
41. Robert M. Hutchins, "Radio and Public Policy," *Education By Radio*, Vol. 4, Number 15 (December 6, 1934): 57.
42. Ibid.: 58.
43. Ibid.: 57.
44. James Rorty, "Order on the Air," *The Nation* (May 9, 1934): 531–32.
45. Kerwin, *The Control of Radio*, p. 8.
46. Ibid., p. 10.
47. Horst J.P. Bergmeier and Rainer E. Lotz, *Hitler's Airwaves: The Inside Story of Nazi Radio Broadcasting and Propaganda Swing* (New Haven: Yale University Press, 1997), p. 6.
48. Ibid., p. 9.
49. Paul Hutchinson, "Education and the Radio," *Christian Century* (April 8, 1931): 478.
50. Rorty, "Order on the Air," *The Nation*: 530.
51. Stephen Lovell, "Broadcasting Bolshevik: The Radio Voice of Soviet Culture, 1920s–1950s," *Journal of Contemporary History* 48, No. 1 (2012): 83.
52. Stephen Lovell, "How Russia Learned to Listen: Radio and the Making of Soviet Culture," *Kritika*, Vol. 12, Number 3 (Summer 2011): 592.
53. Ibid.: 600.
54. Ibid.: 599, 602.

55. Mary S. Mander, "The Public Debate about Broadcasting in the Twenties: An Interpretive History," *Journal of Broadcasting*, Vol. 28, No. 2 (Spring 1984): 183.
56. Lovell, "How Russia Learned to Listen: Radio and the Making of Soviet Culture," *Kritika*: 612.
57. Lovell, "Broadcasting Bolshevik: The Radio Voice of Soviet Culture, 1920s–1950s," *Journal of Contemporary History*: 84, 89.
58. Kerwin, *The Control of Radio*, p. 11.
59. Oscar G. Chase, "Public Broadcasting and the Problem of Government Influence: Towards a Legislative Solution," *University of Michigan Journal of Law Reform* 62 (1975): 64.
60. Kerwin, *The Control of Radio*, p. 24.
61. Ibid., pp. 16, 27.
62. Ibid., p. 26.
63. Gibson, *Public Broadcasting: The Role of the Federal Government, 1912–1976*, p. 16.
64. Walker, *Rebels on the Air: An Alternative History of Radio in America*, p. 37.
65. James A. Brown, "Struggle Against Commercialism: The 1934 'Harney Lobby' for Nonprofit Frequency Allocations," *Journal of Broadcasting & Electronic Media*, Vol. 33, Number 3 (Summer 1989): 279.
66. McChesney, "The Battle for the U.S. Airwaves, 1928–1935," *Journal of Communication*: 35–36.
67. Ibid.: 38–39.
68. Ibid.: 40.
69. Rinks, "Higher Education in Radio, 1922–1934," *Journal of Radio Studies*: 310.
70. Emord, *Freedom, Technology, and the First Amendment*, p. 185.
71. See Milton Mueller, "Property Rights in Radio Communication: The Key to Reform of Telecommunications Regulation," Cato Policy Analysis No. 11, June 3, 1982.
72. McChesney, "Franklin Roosevelt, His Administration, and the Communications Act of 1934," *American Journalism*: 206.
73. Brown, "Struggle Against Commercialism: The 1934 'Harney Lobby' for Nonprofit Frequency Allocations," *Journal of Broadcasting & Electronic Media*: 276.
74. Ibid.: 280.
75. Ibid.: 281–82.
76. Ibid.: 279.
77. Ibid.: 283.
78. Robert W. McChesney, "Crusade Against Mammon: Father Harney, WLWL and the Debate Over Radio in the 1930s," *Journalism History* 14, No. 4 (Winter 1987): 127.
79. Ibid.: 124.
80. Ibid.: 121, 126.
81. Ibid.: 124.

82. Robert W. McChesney, "Labor and the Marketplace of Ideas: WCFL and the Battle for Labor Radio Broadcasting, 1927–1934," *Journalism Monographs* 134 (August 1992): 2.

83. "E.N. Nockels, Labor Leader, Dies Suddenly," *Chicago Tribune*, February 28, 1937.

84. McChesney, "Labor and the Marketplace of Ideas: WCFL and the Battle for Labor Radio Broadcasting, 1927–1934," *Journalism Monographs*: 10.

85. Ralph Engelman, *Public Radio and Television in America: A Political History* (Thousand Oaks, CA: SAGE Publications, 1996), p. 29.

86. McChesney, "Labor and the Marketplace of Ideas: WCFL and the Battle for Labor Radio Broadcasting, 1927–1934," *Journalism Monographs*: 13.

87. Carl J. Friedrich and Evelyn Sternberg, "Congress and the Control of Radio Broadcasting, I," *American Political Science Review*, Vol. XXXVII, No. 5 (October 1943): 802.

88. Brown, "Struggle Against Commercialism: The 1934 'Harney Lobby' for Nonprofit Frequency Allocations," *Journal of Broadcasting & Electronic Media*: 277.

89. McChesney, "The Battle for the U.S. Airwaves, 1928–1935," *Journal of Communication*: 42–43.

90. McChesney, "Franklin Roosevelt, His Administration, and the Communications Act of 1934," *American Journalism*: 204.

91. Friedrich and Sternberg opine that Wagner-Hatfield "was defeated, not so much because Congressmen objected to educational and religious broadcasting, but chiefly because of the faulty drafting of the amendment and the administrative difficulties envisaged in carrying out the particular plan proposed." Friedrich and Sternberg, "Congress and the Control of Radio Broadcasting, I," *American Political Science Review*: 815.

92. Robert K. Avery, "The Public Broadcasting Act of 1967: Radio's Real Second Chance," *Journal of Radio & Audio Media* 24, No. 2 (November 2017): 192.

93. McChesney, "Crusade Against Mammon: Father Harney, WLWL and the Debate Over Radio in the 1930s," *Journalism History*: 128.

94. "A 5-Point Plan for Radio," *New York Times*, October 28, 1934.

95. Arthur E. Morgan, "Radio as a Cultural Agency in Sparsely Settled Regions and Remote Areas," *Education By Radio*, Vol. 4, Number 8 (July 19, 1934): 29.

96. Ibid.: 30.

97. Ibid.: 31.

98. Brown, "Struggle Against Commercialism: The 1934 'Harney Lobby' for Nonprofit Frequency Allocations," *Journal of Broadcasting & Electronic Media*: 285.

99. S.E. Frost Jr., *Education's Own Stations: The History of Broadcast Licenses Issued to Educational Institutions* (Chicago: University of Chicago Press, 1937), p. vi.

Chapter 3
Radio is Good for You! The Rise of Educational Radio

Between 1921 and 1936, 202 broadcast licenses were issued to 168 educational institutions, from Alabama Polytechnic to William Hood Dunwoody Industrial Institute of Minneapolis. The list, as compiled in S.E. Frost Jr.'s encyclopedic *Education's Own Stations* (1937), fairly sings the diversity of America. It includes schools big and small, famous and obscure, urban and rural. They are Antioch and the University of Utah, Yankton and St. Norbert, Iowa State and Cleveland High School, Cornell and the Palmer School of Chiropractic, Rollins and Ruffner Junior High School of Norfolk, Virginia, and Louisiana State and the Moody Bible Institute. Technical, agricultural, and land-grant colleges and universities are perhaps overrepresented; elite Eastern private schools are scarce. Harvard, Yale, and Princeton are absent, but the South Dakota School of Mines, Kansas State College of Agriculture and Applied Sciences, and Ohio State University are present and accounted for.

By January 1, 1937, just 38 of these licenses remained in the hands of educational institutions. The others, as Frost wrote, had been "permitted to expire, transferred to other interests, or revoked by the licensing authority."[1] Some had been sold to commercial broadcasters, others had been abandoned. The stampede away from educational broadcasting had left the field sparse. But were they pushed out or was the medium just not a congenial one for educators?

New York University, to take one example, produced 80 feature programs for New York's station WOR in 1928–29, but this number dropped precipitously in 1930, as the commercial station sold coveted time slots to advertising agencies and the clients they served.[2] There was also the matter of duplication, or co-optation. The big commercial networks, NBC and CBS, encroached upon the preserve of many college and university stations by relaying information and feature stories produced by the U.S. Department of Agriculture. This effectively eroded the perceived need for educational stations, which in some regards now seemed to be duplicating the offerings of commercial stations. (These two networks had within their coteries just over 6% of stations in 1927; four years later, 30% of stations had joined NBC or CBS as affiliates.[3]).

© The Author(s), under exclusive license to Springer Nature Switzerland AG 2021   29
J. T. Bennett, *The History and Politics of Public Radio*, Studies in Public Choice 41,
https://doi.org/10.1007/978-3-030-80019-2_3

A report to the U.S. Secretary of the Interior by the National Advisory Committee on Education by Radio stated that the 77 colleges and universities which owned and operated radio stations in 1930 (12.3% of the total number of stations) broadcast for an average of just eight hours a week. Commercial stations, by contrast, broadcast for an average of 57 h per week, of which about seven and a half hours were devoted to educational matter. Thus, the commercial stations dedicated approximately the same amount of time to the intentional edification of their audience as did those stations expressly created for that purpose. To be fair, the college stations were also hampered by "unfavorable dial positions, low power and unpopular hours on the air," none of which was conducive to a wide listenership.[4]

The rather doleful lesson of the first decade or so of point-to-mass radio was that "the stations owned and operated by colleges and universities have almost no influence," as Paul Hutchinson wrote in *The Christian Century*. Hutchinson explained: "....[I]t can be said that colleges, having constructed broadcasting outfits in their physics laboratories during the early years of the industry, rushed into the field without any clear idea as to what they intended to do; that the hit-or-miss type of program provided failed to gather or hold a large audience, and consequently to command the service of competent broadcasters; that many of these stations became mere propaganda agencies for the enrolment of students or, in more instances, for influencing legislatures to maintain or increase appropriations; and that in the few cases in which college radio stations have built up an extensive clientele it has been mainly by providing important agricultural bulletins, in some cases in conjunction with the federal department of agriculture at Washington."[5] (This last item was a reference to the USDA Radio Service, which supplied agricultural updates and recommendations to such stations, particularly the land-grant schools.)

In his autopsy to determine the cause of the "high mortality rate for stations operated by institutions of higher education," J. Wayne Rinks of the Scripps Howard Center for Media Studies at the University of Southern Indiana cited the imposition of difficult-to-meet technical standards by the federal government, budgetary constraints on some less prosperous schools, and unaffordable music royalty rates demanded by the American Society of Composers, Artists and Performers (ASCAP) beginning in 1923. Some college stations became inaudible in the din of larger commercial stations; others, reduced to limited-hour daytime operation by the FRC and FCC, simply faded away for lack of interest by faculty or students, not to mention potential but never-realized listeners.[6]

The process, which has been dubbed "squeezing the 'long-hairs' out of the picture," generally featured a combination of hardships: an assignment to an outer ghetto frequency; the piling up of difficult-to-meet regulatory requirements; expensive trips to Washington to plead one's case before the Federal Radio Commission or the Federal Communications Commission and to pay mounting legal fees; and the diminution of active hours, which were transferred to commercial stations. Broadcasting historian Werner J. Severin has examined case studies of this squeezing-out. For instance, 9YD, the trailblazing Nebraska Wesleyan University station which took the call letters WCAJ, found itself suddenly sharing time with Omaha's excitingly named WOW in 1928. WOW petitioned to take over the frequency full-time;

unable or unwilling to spend the necessary legal fees against a better-endowed foe, Nebraska Wesleyan sold the station to WOW in 1933, giving the quietus to the weather-forecasting pioneer. Similar stories were played out at schools from Carleton College in Northfield, Minnesota, to the University of Arkansas. The desert fathers of early AM educational radio died off en masse; by 1946, just two educational AM stations were broadcasting after sunset.[7]

By 1937, the number of educational stations had shrunk to 38, as commercial stations assumed their frequencies. But the increasingly dormant genre was given new life, or potential life, when in 1940–41 the FCC approved FM broadcasting and allocated five channels to educational broadcasters. In 1945, the FM band of 88–108 megahertz was established, with the 20 channels located between 88 and 92 MHz reserved for educational broadcasters. The FCC clarified three years later that these stations could broadcast at power levels as low as 10 watts, a Mom and Pop provision that would greatly irritate the larger NPR stations in later years.

Postwar, the FCC was also giving a boost to a medium that would soon overshadow radio, and even threaten to make it seem obsolete, old-fashioned, fuddy-duddy: television. In 1952, the FCC set aside 242 channels for educational television, though four years later just 24, or less than 10%, were up and running.[8] With the advent of television, the efforts of the megabucks foundations such as Ford shifted to the glamorous new medium and away from stodgy old radio. The hopes and dreams of the uplifters, or at least many of those who controlled the purse strings of the nation's great foundations, shifted to the rectangular picture box that came to dominate American living rooms and the waking, non-school hours of so many American children. The prospects for educational television just seemed so much brighter and more glamorous than for radio. The college-affiliated stations in this pre-1960s era were marked by earnestness and amateurishness, which can be an endearing combination, appealingly authentic, but not the kind of thing that appeals or is endearing to foundation executives who want to change the world.

Many of the school radio stations went silent during the summer months or at vacation time; commercial broadcasters shook their heads at such a waste of frequency. The Top 40 hits and frenetic DJ chatter that would mark the resurgent radio of the rock and roll era were all but absent from these stations. To the extent that music seeped from their channels, it was in the form of classical. As Jack W. Mitchell, author of *Listener Supported: The Culture and History of Public Radio*, writes, university-connected stations deployed their "faculties for talks on a variety of topics," from "astronomy to zoology and… backyard agronomy to Zen meditation."[9] None dared call it treason at that time, though many called it boring. Others, however, saw tremendous untapped potential in these sleepy, often sleep-inducing, stations.

In 1950, the Kellogg Foundation subsidized the Tape Network of the National Association of Educational Broadcasters (NAEB), which supplied recorded programs to member stations from its headquarters in Urbana, Illinois. It acted as a clearinghouse, not a production center, duplicating and distributing programs for which members paid a fee based on their budget and power. Subject categories for its approximately 1,500 weekly tapes included "current information, physical sciences, arts and literature, social sciences, mental and physical health, music, and children's programs."[10] In 1964, NAEB created a 150-or-so member National Educational Radio (NER) division, which incorporated the Tape Network. Ominously, to those who feared the politicization of the sector, NER was headquartered in Washington, DC, and authorized to, among other functions, act as "liaison with appropriate government agencies and the Congress."[11] Jerrold Sandler, whom we will meet soon, would prove an effective advocate in this regard.

The NAEB, or more specifically its legal counsel Leonard Marks, hatched the idea that became the Educational Television Facilities Act of 1962. Marks, who was also—significantly—Senator Lyndon B. Johnson's communications attorney, had proposed in 1956 that the federal government assist in the development of educational television facilities. Six years later, with his boss now the Vice President of the United States, Marks's vision concretized. The 1962 act, whose most influential legislative sponsor was Senator Warren Magnuson (D-WA), authorized $32 million over five years in matching grants to the states "to aid in the development of educational television."[12] (It was later amended to include radio facilities.) The program started small: in fiscal year 1963, less than $1 million was dispensed to five recipients in Illinois, South Carolina, Virginia, and Utah. But under President Johnson, the program expanded, as appropriations increased and the federal match was boosted to 75%.[13]

The program would be transferred from the Department of Health, Education, and Welfare to the Department of Commerce and eventually renamed the Public Telecommunications Facilities Program (PTFP), where it largely avoided controversy, as it was a bricks-and-mortar, or recording studio and satellite, affair. Even the Nixon administration, the most determined foe public broadcasting would meet, gave it a free pass, as Michael W. Huntsberger details in his account of the short and relatively placid life of the PTFP.

The proposed budgets of Presidents Ronald Reagan and George H.W. Bush zeroed out the program, not for any ideological reason but because it was felt to have outlived its purpose. While appropriations would diminish after hitting a peak of $24 million in FY 1980, reauthorizations continued, and during the Clinton administration, the PTFP assisted public radio and television stations with their conversion to digital transmission. Once this was accomplished, the Obama administration put the quietus to the program, with the director of the Office of Management and Budget singling it out as "plainly wasteful and duplicative."[14] In all, the facilities act, under whatever name, "distributed more than $800 million to support the construction of public broadcasting facilities" between 1963 and its termination in 2010.[15]

The Educational Television Facilities Act was a counterattack on what FCC Chairman Newton Minow had called in 1961 the "vast wasteland" of commercial television, a "procession of game shows, formula comedies about totally unbelievable families, blood and thunder, mayhem, violence, sadism, murder, western bad men, western good men, private eyes, gangsters, more violence, and cartoons."[16] (The man who appointed Minow, President John F. Kennedy, may well have been watching one of those entries he disparaged that very evening.)

So, the focus at elite levels had shifted to television. Radio as a forum for a wide, invigorating, even enraging variety of views was hardly a mainstream ideal among the nation's decision-makers of the 1950s and'60s. But just as the early architects of government propaganda had viewed the airwaves as potentially useful conduits, so did their heirs in the Cold War era. The influential political scientist Harold Laswell of Yale, in a 1952 lecture to the convention of the National Association of Educational Broadcasters, framed the question in this way: "How to capture the gadgets of modern society for the service of our basic moral and political ideas"?[17] Radio and the other tools of the communication revolution of the twentieth century should be used "to bind men together for the achievement of positive moral and social values," argued Lasswell, whose examples of such values tended to be conterminous with the agenda of the U.S. government decision-makers.[18]

As an instance of furthering "public enlightenment," he singled out the need to explain to the hoi polloi "why SHAPE is in Europe."[19] By SHAPE he meant the Supreme Headquarters Allied Power Europe, or the Allied Command Operations of NATO. Lasswell was writing at a time when significant public opposition, coming from both right and left, existed to the deployment of U.S. troops in Europe. Whether motivated by peace sentiments or old-fashioned American isolationism, substantial public figures, as well as millions of ordinary Americans, wanted to keep U.S. troops home. So educational broadcasters, suggested Lasswell, could take it upon themselves to instruct listeners in the reasons for U.S. military engagement in Europe and present a favorable view of the NATO alliance. (The failure of NPR, even today, 30 years after the fall of the Soviet Union, to give any appreciable airtime to contemporary critics of NATO or advocates of U.S. military retrenchment would, one supposes, warm Lasswell's heart.)

Similarly, Lasswell urged the broadcasters to employ "[c]ommunications experts" to break down economic theories for the layman. Specifically, how to "financ[e] a major war effort with a minimum of immediate or eventual disruption of living standards."[20] Thus radio could be used to popularize technocratic plans for the Cold War liberal economy. Looking ahead, Lasswell forecast the development of "Public Service Communicators" to explicate complicated political and social concepts for the masses.[21] It was the manufacture of consent in plain sight.

While Harold Lasswell's ex cathedra pronouncements from on high remained mostly in the airy realm of theory, an idealistic and ideologically variegated group of activists on the West Coast were demonstrating the potential of radio to explore complex issues, to delve into philosophical and political questions, and to bring culture to the listeners. And they were showing that government subsidy need not be the lifeblood of a radio station that aspired beyond Top 40 hits, inane chatter, or conventional news programming.

This example of the potential of privately supported educational radio was provided by Lewis Hill, the visionary behind Berkeley-based Pacifica Radio. Hill, whose maternal uncle was the founder of Phillips Petroleum, was a Missouri-bred Quaker pacifist and Washington, DC, correspondent who in 1946 set out to put into practice his dream of a listener-supported radio station where artists and thinkers would be welcome. The name Pacifica was a nod to his pacifist leanings, not the ocean of which the nearby San Francisco Bay is an estuary. It took Hill three years to raise the necessary $15,000 in startup funds; Uncle Frank the oil baron was obviously not a major sponsor. The model, as Pacifica's Eleanor McKinney remembered in 1962, was not condescending lectures from "all us bright people in here broadcasting to all you sheep-type masses out there," but rather addressing listeners as "people of intelligence" who wanted to hear live concerts, vigorous debates, children's programs, and discussions of literature and public affairs that included "majority viewpoints and minority views seldom or never heard on radio."[22] Everyone from communists to members of the far right had their say on Pacifica—a stark contrast to the NPR model, in which the range of permissible opinion stretches from Mitt Romney to Kamala Harris. As Jesse Walker writes, "Pacifica was founded by libertarians, sort of"—by men and women of the left, to be sure, but "a more individualist and anti-statist left than listeners familiar with the network's current incarnation might expect."[23]

Volunteers helped outfit the modest studio of Pacifica's flagship, Berkeley-based station KPFA, which went on the air, fittingly, on April 15, 1949: Tax Day. For this was a venture that relied not on coercion or the state-directed transfer of funds but on good old-fashioned American voluntarism. All members of the small staff received the same salary, though gestures toward a similar egalitarianism with regard to running the station proved impractical, and Hill was clearly first among equals.

The anarchistic Hill rejected both the commercial model and the idea of government assistance; his idea, as his admirer the social psychologist Erich Fromm wrote, was that Pacifica's listeners "would voluntarily subscribe to exceptional radio programs just as they subscribe to newspapers and magazines; that they would pay this voluntary fee even though they could hear the broadcasts for nothing."[24] To survive financially, Lewis Hill believed, the station would need to attract donations from "2 per cent of the total FM audience in the area in which it operates."[25] This proved overly ambitious. When money got tight, the hosts admitted the dearth—and their grateful listeners came to the rescue. A couple of years into the experiment, the Fund for Adult Education of the Ford Foundation, impressed by the avid response of Pacifica's listening community, came through with a three-year, $150,000 grant.[26]

Hill disparaged most contemporary radio as mediocre or designed simply to sell products, not encourage the intelligent discussion of ideas. He scorned educational radio as boring and unwilling to challenge the status quo, remarking that "the people in charge of educational stations are tied either to state legislatures or to boards of trustees which inevitably represent tendencies close to the commercial and conservative part of the community."[27] Hill stressed that he was not promoting a "Down with Commerce" attitude, but rather trying to fashion a funding system that, because it relied on voluntary contributions by people who valued the station's offerings, encouraged excellence.[28]

Although situated on the left end of the political spectrum, not to mention the dial, Pacifica welcomed a broad range of opinions emanating from everyone from members of the Communist Party to activists of the John Birch Society. It played host to folk singers and activists, philosophers and artists, community leaders and troublemakers. It welcomed controversy. Poets Allen Ginsberg and Kenneth Rexroth and movie critic Pauline Kael spoke over its airwaves, as did conservatives such as *National Review* editor William F. Buckley Jr. and future Reagan Secretary of Defense Caspar Weinberger.[29]

Lewis Hill, who suffered from spinal arthritis, committed suicide, perhaps due to a combination of physical pain and organizational tumult, at the tender age of 38 in 1957; two years later, KPFA's first sister station, KPFK of Los Angeles, went on the air. A year later, a commercial station in New York City, WBAI, was gifted to Pacifica by its owner, Louis Schweitzer. The stations subsisted on a mixture of $15 annual "subscriptions" (for which the donor received a program guide), bequests, and grants.[30]

The best description of how WBAI came under the Pacifica fold was sketched by Jesse Walker, the excellent libertarian journalist and alternative radio maven. Writes Walker:

> WBAI began as an ordinary commercial station in 1955, broadcasting at 99.5 FM. Then an eccentric millionaire named Louis Schweitzer bought it, thinking this would be a good way to ensure he could hear more classical music on the radio. The station got an unexpected boost in listenership during a newspaper strike, as New Yorkers tuned to it for the news, and Schweitzer found he had a financial success on his hands. Unfortunately for Schweitzer, that meant he was hearing more commercials on his station—and he hated listening to ads. So he decided to hand the whole thing over to the Pacifica Foundation, which had been broadcasting a mixture of highbrow cultural programming and dissident political commentary in Berkeley, California, since 1949 and had just launched a second station in Los Angeles.
>
> So Schweitzer cold-called Harold Winkler, Pacifica's president, and told him that he could have WBAI if he wanted it. Much of the ensuing conversation reportedly consisted of Schweitzer trying to convince Winkler that he was not a crank—or, at least, that he was a very rich crank who really did intend to give away a radio station. The transaction was soon completed, and in 1960 WBAI became a noncommercial Pacifica station broadcasting in the middle of New York's commercial FM band.[31]

Its openness to radical points of view led to Pacifica's then-president, Hallock Hoffman, being hauled before the U.S. Senate's Internal Security Subcommittee in 1963. The Federal Communications Commission was threatening to reject the renewal of the licenses for Pacifica's then-three stations. Pacifica spokesmen insisted that "the only way to preserve … freedom is by practicing it," and so they offered a spirited defense of their freewheeling style.[32] In January 1964, the FCC roundly defended the right of stations to offer provocative programming. In renewing the Pacifica licenses, the FCC decision stated that some material on Pacifica stations "may offend some listeners. But this does not mean that those offended have the right, through the Commission's licensing power, to rule such programming off the airwaves. Were this the case, only the wholly inoffensive, the bland, could gain access to the radio microphone or TV camera."[33]

On a parallel path, Lorenzo Milam, a Floridian who had volunteered at Lewis Hill's KPFA, became known widely as the Johnny Appleseed of community radio for his creative and energetic seeding of more than a dozen such stations across the country, most notably his cherished KRAB-FM in Seattle, whose "varied schedule made Pacifica look tame," as Jesse Walker writes. In the 1960s, KRAB would place reports "from the front lines of the civil rights struggle" cheek by jowl with a program produced by the segregationist White Citizens' Council.[34] KRAB subsisted on monies begged from fund-raising drives and Milam's modest wealth. It was anti-authority, anti-bureaucracy, and very much in an anarchist rather than a socialist vein.

It lasted twenty-two years before going dark. Its archivist writes, by way of obituary, that its founders and supporters "naïvely believed that there were, are, enough people like themselves, intellectually curious, artistically adventuresome, open and willing to be challenged by political views contrary to their own, and believers in the power of communication to improve society, so that a radio station not serving commercial interests could be financially viable. That thesis continues to be tested."[35]

Non-commercial, non-governmental radio, often dubbed *community radio* by its admirers, was distinguished by its absence of advertising, its stated intention to democratize the airwaves and open them up to voices previously unheard, and its reliance on voluntary support, both financial and in staffing. It prized "citizen participation and a healthy diversity of opinion," and this was not necessarily meaningless boilerplate: for instance, Pacifica's WBAI featured commentary from the anti-collectivist novelist Ayn Rand, among other figures usually associated with the political Right.[36] But for the most part, these stations skewed left, and left was defined as closer to the dissident fringe (socialist, pacifist, black nationalist) than, say, Adlai Stevensonian liberalism. Over the decades, one by one, community radio stations have thrown in with National Public Radio, preferring a reliable source of funding, even if it comes with government strings attached, to the uncertainty of true independence. The "hippie paradigm" which the professionals mocked was the road to penury.

Yet as Jesse Walker writes, although community radio "may be the only noncommercial radio in this country that is truly 'public,' relying on local volunteers for most of its programming, financial support, and day-to-day administration," the Corporation for Public Broadcasting (CPB) "has been wary of community stations' localism, experimentalism, and volunteer base," as it has sought, almost since its birth, to "replace the scattered array of small stations with a tighter, more centralized public radio system under professional control."[37] As Walker notes, accepting monies from the national government has the seemingly inevitable effect of lessening a station's localist angle of vision and bringing it into line with all the other federally subsidized nodes of the national network.

The "community service grants" which the CPB today ships to NPR affiliates and offers to community stations are not string-free. They carry standards for paid staffing, power, hours of operation, listenership, and finances. Accepting such grants alters the nature of grass roots community radio stations, which is why many consider them a gilded trap. The incentive impels one toward a philosophy, and practice, of Get Big—or at least bigger—or get out. Alas, as shown later, Pacifica eventually succumbed to the lure of federal dollars and a more conventional leftist outlook. The seeds of its surrender were sown by the very establishment against which it had once set its cap.

Not every community broadcaster has thrown in with Washington; others regard it as Mordor. Stephen Dunifer, the anarchist founder of Radio Free Berkley and a pioneer in the low-power field of microradio, calls the CPB "the Agent Orange of grassroots radio."[38] (For the story of microradio in all its ragged glory, see Jesse Walker's excellent 2001 book *Rebels on the Air: An Alternative History of Radio in America*.) And WFMU-FM of East Orange, New Jersey, formerly associated with

Upsala College but now independent, is funded wholly by private donations and, due to its adventurous musical offerings, has on multiple occasions been named "Best Radio Station" in America by *Rolling Stone* magazine.

Notes of Chapter

1.   Frost, *Education's Own Stations: The History of Broadcast Licenses Issued to Educational Institutions*, p. 3.
2.   Rosen, *The Modern Stentors: Radio Broadcasters and the Federal Government, 1920–1934*, p. 166.
3.   McChesney, "The Battle for the U.S. Airwaves, 1928–1935," *Journal of Communication*: 33.
4.   Paul Hutchinson, "Education and the Radio," *Christian Century* (April 8, 1931): 479.
5.   Ibid.: 480.
6.   Rinks, "Higher Education in Radio, 1922–1934," *Journal of Radio Studies*: 303, 314.
7.   Severin, "Commercial v. Non-Commercial Radio During Broadcasting's Early Years," *Journal of Broadcasting*: 497–98, 502.
8.   John Edward Burke, *An Historical-Analytical Study of the Legislative and Political Origins of the Public Broadcasting Act of 1967* (New York: Arno Press, 1979) p. 29.
9.   Jack W. Mitchell, *Listener Supported: The Culture and History of Public Radio* (Westport, CT: Praeger, 2005), p. 18.
10. Herman W. Land Associates, *The Hidden Medium: A Status Report on Educational Radio in the United States* (New York: Herman W. Land Associates, 1967), pp. I–23.
11. Jerrold Sandler, Introduction, *The Hidden Medium: A Status Report on Educational Radio in the United States*, p. ii.
12. Burke, *An Historical-Analytical Study of the Legislative and Political Origins of the Public Broadcasting Act of 1967*, p. 51.
13. Michael W. Huntsberger, "Attempting an Affirmation Approach to American Broadcasting: Ideology, Politics, and the Public Telecommunications Facilities Program," *Journalism & Mass Communication Quarterly*, Vol. 91, No. 4 (2014): 761.
14. Ibid.: 765.
15. Ibid.: 756.
16. Newton N. Minow, "Television and the Public Interest," speech to the National Association of Broadcasters, May 9, 1961, www.americanrhetoric.com.
17. Harold Lasswell, "Educational Broadcasters as Social Scientists," *The Quarterly of Film, Radio, and Television*, Vol. 7, No. 2 (Winter 1952): 150. The National Association of Educational Broadcasters, or NAEB, was so denominated in 1934; it had previously been the Association of College and University Broadcasting Stations.
18. Ibid.: 151.

19. Ibid.: 153.
20. Ibid.: 158.
21. Ibid.: 162.
22. Eleanor McKinney, "About Pacifica Radio, Broadcast 1962," *The Exacting Ear: The Story of Listener-Sponsored Radio, and an Anthology of Programs from KPFA, KPFK, and WBAI* (New York: Pantheon, 1966), pp. 11, 13.
23. Jesse Walker, "Another War Breaks Out in the Pacifica Radio Network," reason.com, March 19, 2014.
24. Erich Fromm, Preface, *The Exacting Ear: The Story of Listener-Sponsored Radio, and an Anthology of Programs from KPFA, KPFK, and WBAI*, p. 4.
25. Lewis Hill, "The Theory of Listener-Sponsored Radio," in ibid., p. 25.
26. McKinney, "About Pacifica Radio, Broadcast 1962," *The Exacting Ear: The Story of Listener-Sponsored Radio, and an Anthology of Programs from KPFA, KPFK, and WBAI*, p. 14.
27. Engelman, *Public Radio and Television in America: A Political History*, p. 44.
28. Hill, "The Theory of Listener-Sponsored Radio," *The Exacting Ear: The Story of Listener-Sponsored Radio, and an Anthology of Programs from KPFA, KPFK, and WBAI*, p. 23.
29. Walker, "Another War Breaks Out in the Pacifica Radio Network," reason.com.
30. Herman W. Land Associates, *The Hidden Medium: A Status Report on Educational Radio in the United States*, p. SP-12.
31. Jesse Walker, "The Possibly Pending Death of a Legendary Radio Station," Reason, October 18, 2019, www.reason.com.
32. *The Exacting Ear: The Story of Listener-Sponsored Radio, and an Anthology of Programs from KPFA, KPFK, and WBAI*, p. 320.
33. Ibid., p. 322.
34. Walker, *Rebels on the Air: An Alternative History of Radio in America*, p. 70.
35. "KRAB-FM 107.7 Seattle, Washington 1962–1984," http://www.krabarchive.com/.
36. William Barlow, "Community radio in the US: the struggle for a democratic medium," *Media, Culture and Society*, Vol. 10 (1988): 82.
37. Jesse Walker, "With Friends Like These: Why Community Radio Does Not Need the Corporation for Public Broadcasting," Cato Institute, Policy Analysis No. 277, July 24, 1997.
38. Ibid.

Chapter 4
Carnegie's Lemon? The Birth of NPR

Television, the archenemy of radio, provided the cover under which educational radio went on the federal payroll. In December 1964, a National Conference on Long-Range Financing of ETV (educational television) convened, encouragingly or ominously, depending upon your predilections, in Washington, DC. Largely underwritten by the U.S. Office of Education under the National Defense Education Act and cosponsored by the National Association of Educational Broadcasters, the more than 260 attendees at the two-day conference heard from, among others, FCC Chairman E. William Henry, who told the conferees that a "giant" task of educational television was to overcome the "electronic Appalachia"—the "cultural poverty" of America which commercial TV had left untouched.[1] The slight against Appalachia, whose cultural riches, especially musically, dwarf those of many wealthier regions, passed by unremarked.

Bedazzled by the possibilities of greatly increased federal involvement in edifying television, the conferees issued a series of mandates, the capstone of which was a demand for "the appointment of a Presidential Commission" to make recommendations toward the expansion of their field.[2] Specifically, they desired the commission "to study the financial needs of educational television and the manner in which they might be met."[3] This led to the birth of the Carnegie Commission on Educational Television, a blue-ribbon establishmentarian panel sponsored by the Carnegie Corporation of New York and given the task to "conduct a broadly conceived study of noncommercial television" and to "focus its attention principally, although not exclusively, on commonly-owned channels and their services to the general public.... The Commission will recommend lines along which noncommercial television stations might most usefully develop during the years ahead."[4]

Despite the aegis of Carnegie, this was, from the first, a federal government-driven project. Carnegie Corporation President John Gardner, soon to be made U.S. Secretary of Health, Education, and Welfare, energetically supported the proposal, as did Vice President Hubert Humphrey, FCC Chairman Henry, and others, and the commission was born. Its 15 members, all personally approved by President Johnson, included current and former university presidents (chairman James R. Killian Jr. of the Massachusetts Institute of Technology; James B. Conant of Harvard; Lee A. DuBridge of the California Institute of Technology; David D. Henry of Illinois; and Franklin Patterson of Hampshire College); titans of business (presidents Edwin H. Land of Polaroid and Joseph H. McConnell of Reynolds Metals); a union leader (Leonard Woodcock of the United Auto Workers); media executives (Oveta Culp Hobby, chairman of the board of the *Houston Post;* and J.C. Kellam, president of the Texas Broadcasting Corporation—both Texans, you will notice, as was the president of the United States, Lyndon B. Johnson: quelle coincidence!); politicos (former North Carolina Governor Terry Sanford and John S. Hayes, Johnson's ambassador to Switzerland and a former official of the *Washington Post*; John Burke—whose Ph.D. thesis concerned the conception, development, and eventual enactment of the Public Broadcasting Act of 1967—writes that Hayes was chosen because his participation "would lead to public support through the *Washington Post*"[5]); television producer Robert Saudek; and, lastly, two real-life artists: Ralph Ellison, best known for his classic work *Invisible Man*, and concert pianist Rudolf Serkin.

Over the course of a year, and supported by a $500,000 grant from Carnegie, the Carnegie Commission on Educational Television held eight formal meetings. It also took testimony, in person and in writing, from over 225 persons and organizations, and its members and staff visited 92 educational TV stations in 35 different states.[6] No testimony exceeded in its grandiloquence or daffy optimism a September 26, 1966, letter from the great essayist E.B. White. Written on *New Yorker* stationery, White's missive saw in television the potential to be "the visual counterpart of the literary essay." The boob tube "should arouse our dreams, satisfy our hunger for beauty, take us on journeys, enable us to participate in events, present great drama and music, explore the sea and the sky and the woods and the hills. It should be our Lyceum, our Chautauqua, our Minsky's, and our Camelot. It should restate and clarify the social dilemma and the political pickle."[7] Evidently, Mr. White was dissatisfied with *Gilligan's Island*. He was laying it on thick here, and if his tongue was not planted at least partially in cheek then he must otherwise have been well into his cups. But there really was, in some quarters, a belief in the luminous potential of public broadcasting. Now if only a revenue source could be dug up….

The educational television of that pre-PBS day consisted primarily of stations affiliated with colleges and universities and other institutions of learning, and which offered students the chance at hands-on experience à la college radio. Of much greater fame, or notoriety to some, National Educational Television (NET), a Ford Foundation-supported entity which was not federally subsidized, ran "hard-hitting documentaries that challenged the status quo with titles such as *Who Invited the US?*, *The Poor Pay More*, *Black Like Me*, and *Inside North Vietnam*. These were, as the titles suggest, leftist in orientation, but their private funding sources placed them beyond the reach of censorship-minded politicians. As constitutional scholar Trevor Burrus writes, "The dirty secret of public broadcasting is that initially, federal funding was partially given as a way to make the message more palatable to government."[8] After all, the board of what became the Corporation for Public Broadcasting was hand-picked by the President; thus, in theory at least, it would be responsive to pressure from the administration, whether that of Lyndon B. Johnson or Richard M. Nixon.

The Carnegie Commission may have envisioned public television as being "a forum for debate and controversy," but by the infusion of federal monies, this debate and these controversies were, inevitably, circumscribed.[9]

The airing of *Inside North Vietnam*, a film by British documentarian Felix Greene which was originally commissioned but then rejected by CBS, drew a letter of protest to NET president John White from 33 members of Congress, but they had no way to prevent its showing. The letter, whose prime sponsor was former Congressman Walter Judd (R-MN), called *Inside North Vietnam* "nothing more nor less than communist propaganda," despite the fact that, according to historian James Ledbetter, none of the solons had yet seen the film.[10] Many found NET's documentaries to be radical chic, or shallowly leftist, but at least they were being produced by private sources and not on the taxpayer's dime. NET president White was hauled before a closed session of a congressional committee when his network also aired a controversial documentary about Fidel Castro, but he—with the freedom of speech that comes from not accepting federal monies—told the members of Congress that they did not fund him and thus he did not answer to them.[11]

A critic sympathetic to *Inside North Vietnam*, Robert Lewis Shayon of the *Saturday Review of Literature*, thought that the furor over that film was an object lesson in "the importance of funding public TV in such a way that it is not subject to annual Congressional appropriations," yet had NET been a project of the federal government, the heavy hand of censorship likely would have intervened. As Clay Whitehead, who headed up the Nixon administration's Office of Telecommunications Policy, noted in a 1969 memo, the upside of federally funded rather than privately funded educational television was that the administration "could presumably have a hand in picking the head of such a major new organization if it were funded by" the Corporation for Public Broadcasting.[12]

The Carnegie Commission, while not wholly neglecting university-affiliated television, focused on noncommercial television, which had a potentially much greater reach. Sure, a grainy broadcast of an hour-long lecture by a professor of paleontology over the University of Montana's in-house station was no doubt worthy and edifying and all that, but imagine a nationwide "system that in its totality will become a new and fundamental institution in American culture," beaming to viewers from the Redwood Forests to the Gulf Stream waters high-level productions of classic plays or operas or symphonies and the occasional documentary about, oh, say, just, for example, the ominous threat of Goldwaterism.[13]

The Carnegie Commission released its report in January 1967, more or less coincident with President Johnson's declaration in his 1967 State of the Union address that "We should develop educational television into a vital public resource to enrich our homes, educate our families, and to provide assistance in our classrooms. We should insist that the public interest be fully served through our nation's airwaves."[14] The report posited that the development of a "well-financed and well-directed educational television system, substantially larger and far more pervasive and effective than that which now exists in the United States, must be brought into being if the full needs of the American public are to be served."[15] Just how these unmet needs were to be divined would be a matter for elevated minds, or at least politically well-connected ones.

The commission issued twelve recommendations, the centerpiece of which was the federal creation of a Corporation for Public Television, which would "receive and disburse governmental and private funds" to local stations and national production centers, and for purposes including production, programming, the improvement of facilities, technical experimentation, and the recruitment of personnel, among others.[16] Its "principal responsibility" would be "supporting program production."[17] It would be financed by a federal trust fund funded by a manufacturer's excise tax on TV sets, which would be set at 2 percent and rise to a maximum of 5 percent. Amusingly, the commission asserted that TV set purchasers shouldn't mind paying this tax because "the improved service made possible by the tax directly increases the real value of the set." Just think of the resale value of those sets! The federal subsidy of the CPT was proposed to be $40 million in the first year and $60 million per year thereafter.[18]

David Sarnoff, who for many years led the Radio Corporation of America (RCA), had anticipated such a plan back in 1924, when he wrote in *The Nation*, "To tax the public for radio reception would be a reversion, in my belief, to the days of toll roads and bridges, to the days when schools were not free and libraries were not public."[19] In that same year, Senator Dill, the state of Washington Democrat and most influential legislative voice in the communications policy of the era, also spoke against a tax on radio sets, comparing it to a tax on newspapers. Orated Senator Dill: "Just as firmly as I believe that the press ought to be kept free and that speech ought to be kept free, I believe the right to use a radio ought to be kept free because I believe it will eventually be a far greater blessing than the free press has been in this country."[20] The accuracy of his prophecy probably depends on what one thinks of when asked to think of the history of radio in America: the Saturday broadcasts of the Metropolitan Opera brought to you by Texaco, Dr. Demento, Air America, *The Shadow*, Orson Welles's *War of the Worlds*, Dr. Laura, Alan Freed, or listening to the Friday night football game played by one's local high school.

On a parallel, if narrower track, the Carnegie Commission recommended that the U.S. Department of Health, Education, and Welfare assist in the support of the creation, maintenance, and operation of "educational television stations" providing "instructional television programming."[21] These small, often school-run stations, were an afterthought for the Carnegie commissioners, and the report conceded that the "general attitude" of its members "was recognized to be ambivalent."[22] The world-changing possibilities of crop reports and junior-college Algebra 101 courses are limited. Unlike poky instructional television, public television stations would broadcast sufficient "programming … from major national production centers or from stations in the great metropolitan areas to assure that localism within the system will not become parochialism."[23] In other words, any local accents would be drowned out by voices from New York and Washington. Yet the commissioners paid lip service to "the bedrock of localism" upon which the edifice of this national system would ostensibly rest.

The commission briefly acknowledged the potential for political manipulation of a federally subsidized network of television stations, but it blithely assured readers that the Corporation for Public Television would be "free of political interference" because it was somehow "nongovernmental"—despite being created and endowed by the federal government and having its 12-member board of directors appointed by the President and/or the other directors and being confirmed by the Senate.[24] It was as if simply asserting the absence of political interference made it true. The commission earnestly affirmed the dubious claim that because the federal monies directed to the Corporation for Public Television were to be placed in a trust fund rather than appropriated expressly to the recipients, therefore the entire process was pure and immaculate and as far removed from "the dangers of political control" as could be.[25] As if influencing media coverage of his administration was the furthest thing from Lyndon B. Johnson's mind! In the fullness, or briefness, of time, we would be treated to numerous lessons in the impossibility of shielding media recipients of federal monies from political interference.

Rhetoric soared. Sometimes it soared so high that it became almost unrecognizable, turning definitions inside out. With the assassination of President Kennedy still a painful and recent memory, the call to arms rang with Kennedyesque diction. The last two paragraphs of the Carnegie Commission's report echoed JFK:

> If we were to sum up our proposal with all the brevity at our command, we would say that what we recommend is freedom. We seek freedom from the constraints, however necessary in their context, of commercial television. We seek for educational television freedom from the pressures of inadequate funds. We seek for the artist, the technician, the journalist, the scholar, and the public servant freedom to create, freedom to innovate, freedom to be heard in this most far-reaching medium. We seek for the citizen freedom to view, to see programs that the present system, by its incompleteness, denies him.

> Because this freedom is its principal burden, we submit our Report with confidence: to rally the American people in the name of freedom is to ask no more of them than they have always been willing to provide.[26]

This gust of wind, intended to lift hearts, confuses. The only real thing being "asked" of the American people is that they pay higher taxes to subsidize the viewing preferences of the Carnegie Commission members. It is an unusual form of freedom that consists of little beyond yielding a pound of flesh—or a few dollars more, as the financial burden of public television has never been all that heavy. And is American freedom really best exercised by watching television?

Most hilarious is the demand that the "public servant" be granted the "freedom to create, freedom to innovate, freedom to be heard." Most Americans were unaware that their politicians desired creative freedom, much less that they were capable of exercising it. Yes, the occasional actor (Ronald Reagan, George Murphy, Al Franken) takes a stab at politics, and writers (Norman Mailer, Gore Vidal) have occasionally mounted campaigns for public office, though these were more in the way of broadening or enlivening debate rather than achieving political power. Musicians have very rarely attained federal office, though John Hall, singer of the 1970s pop band Orleans, served two terms in Congress from Upstate New York. In each case, the artist had been free to create and innovate before taking office or mounting a campaign, and the implied absence of this freedom in the Carnegie Commission's penultimate paragraph puzzles. But then it's easy to lose one's way in the purple thickets of Kennedyesque rhetoric.

A follow-up report by Carnegie anticipated the twenty-first century buzzword *diversity* by some decades: "The true greatness of America lies in the strength that emerges from this kind of diversity of religious, racial, or cultural heritage. Public broadcasting must create an enterprise that attracts their continuing administration and support if it is to survive and flourish. The revelation of diversity will not please some, notably the book burners and the dogmatists among us. It will startle and anger others, as it should."[27]

Carnegie commissioners were Galileo and John Scopes all rolled into one! The tone of self-righteousness is nigh unbearable; surely the authors all imagine themselves as people who would have stood up to Joe McCarthy. But ideological diversity has been rare from the start in federally funded media, despite the efforts of some of its founders and inspirational figures, and although its staffers have not burned books—that practice is out of favor and has been for the last century in even the most benighted quarters—simply ignoring books that do not fit the overarching narrative is a far more effective way of ensuring uniformity of voice.

The Carnegie Commission ignored radio, which merited not even an afterthought or a thrown bone. But the educational radio community was aware that something big was in the offing and was determined to shoehorn itself into the nascent federal program for public broadcasting. The National Educational Radio division of the National Association of Educational Broadcasters, with a grant from the Ford Foundation (which was severing its alms-giving ties to educational radio in favor of educational television), commissioned Herman W. Land Associates of New York City to prepare the intriguingly titled *The Hidden Medium: A Status Report on Educational Radio in the United States*. The report was issued in April 1967, in the midst of the Johnson administration's legislative reification of the Carnegie Commission's work, though its roots were in a September 1966 conference of educational broadcasters at Racine, Wisconsin, convened by the NER and the Johnson Foundation of Racine. The conferees developed an action plan, the first item of which was a request that further action be subsidized by taxpayers. To wit, "That specific administrative and legislative steps be taken to facilitate public support for educational radio at the federal, state and local levels."[28]

NER's board of directors authorized Herman W. Land, erstwhile editor of *Television* magazine, to document "the true scope of educational radio in the United States." The resulting publication, which was distributed to every member of the U.S. Senate and House of Representatives (though if a single member ever read it the sky might have fallen), would be "needed as a basis for support through legislation and from private sources as well."[29] With Ford Foundation's assistance, Herman Land and the NER attempted to survey the universe of U.S. educational radio licensees. About 40 percent, or 135 of 320, replied to questionnaires, and 50 were interviewed in person and by phone.

Jerrold Sandler, the executive director of NER and a man who would play a critical, if somewhat furtive, role in preparing the airwaves for what became National Public

Radio (NPR), provided a dry introduction to the report, bereft of the soaring rhetoric of the Carnegie production. Briefly sketching the history of educational radio, Sandler made the point that it was no mere afterthought, no minor appendage to the medium, but rather constituted "the core of this country's earliest broadcasting operations."[30]

Herman Land and his associates alternated laments over the sorry state of Great Society-era educational radio with hints, prosaically phrased, of what it might become were it adequately funded. It "has suffered long neglect arising from disinterest [*sic*] and apathy among the educational administrators who control much of its fortunes," the report began. "As a result, it lacks cohesion as a medium, its purposes are varied and often confused, and it struggles for the beginnings of recognition as a potentially valuable national resource."[31] Not exactly a rousing call to action.

The closest the Land crew comes to poetry is perhaps in their vision of what educational radio was, or ought to be: "It is the classical music station which brings the best in music to a locality which otherwise might be without it; the agricultural station which presents but little music, but which is depended upon for expert information about farming; the in-school station that parents listen to so they can know what their child is being taught; the community station that goes out to seek community groups so they can appear on its air waves."[32] This rings anachronistic today. Although the U.S. Department of Agriculture noted proudly in 1965 that educational stations carried fully half of the 800,000 USDA broadcasts that year, agricultural reports are now nigh absent from public radio, which is largely oblivious to the farm population.[33] In-school FM stations are obsolete in the digital era. And NPR affiliates are often embarrassed by their ancient reputation as classical music jukeboxes, an image that seems unhip, stodgy, and, in this era of identity politics, upper-middle-class white in complexion.

In this last vein, the report limns a problem, or what advocates perceived then and now as a problem: namely, that educational radio "serve[s] the needs of those already well endowed with the gifts of time, aptitude and interest for things cultural." The challenge, and the opportunity, was for the medium to "bestir itself on behalf of the special groups within the society, such as the disadvantaged, the elderly, the minorities, etc., for whom it appears uniquely equipped to fill the media vacuum that generally prevails."[34] That this did not happen in 1967, nor is it happening more than half a century later, has not prevented today's partisans and publicists for NPR from saying more or less the same thing.

Much of *The Hidden Medium* consists of an explication of the results from the Herman Land Associates survey questionnaires sent to virtually the entirety of U.S. educational stations (320 of a total of 346). Of this number, 311 were on the FM band (mostly on the left-sided educational band) and 134 of those were low-power (10 W) stations whose signal stretched no more than five miles from its source.[35] The remaining AM stations were primarily run by land-grant colleges whose licenses dated back decades. About 70 percent (244) of the stations were licensed to colleges and universities, with another 51 licensed to public schools. Among other licensees were Bible colleges (10), independent schools (10), and public libraries (3). Geographically, the Northeast, Pacific Northwest, and Great

Lakes were dotted most heavily with such stations, while the Southeast, Southwest, and Rocky Mountain states were more spottily represented.[36]

A large majority of those stations that responded to the survey (114 of 135) operated for at least six hours on weekdays, but less than half of the respondents were active on Saturdays (59) or Sundays (51). Those silent on weekends tended to be in-school stations. Contrary to commercial radio, whose hours of heaviest listenership are in the morning during "drive time," educational radio in the mid-1960s was most active from noon to midnight and far less active in the from 6 to 9 a.m. period.

Budgets of those surveyed were on the modest side. About half survived on less than $20,000 annually, while just one-seventh had yearly budgets above $100,000.[37] Moreover, stations of all sizes were "beset with manpower problems," according to Herman Land Associates, and more than three-quarters of station managers who responded to the survey reported that they lacked adequate staffing.[38] Then again, this is the answer the survey-givers were looking for, and if a respondent believes, accurately, that to plead understaffing increases the likelihood that financial assistance will be boosted, then the answers to the questions write themselves. (Interestingly, the managers who were far and away the most likely to report that their stations were adequately staffed were those helming 10 W stations—perhaps because they understood that federal subsidies would not trickle down to them.[39]) Majorities also claimed to have inadequate or no newsroom facilities and promotional efforts.[40]

Nineteen of the respondents submitted to more detailed questioning. Salient findings included:

- Listenership rose steadily in the early evening hours and peaked at 10 p.m., antipodal to commercial radio.
- Audiences were older, more highly educated, and had larger average incomes than audiences for commercial stations.
- Classical music was the most popular programming format. As the authors, in a rare flash of personality, noted puckishly, "It is often assumed that educational radio stations broadcast long-playing classical records from an inexhaustible collection all day long, occasionally interspersing a news report or recorded lecture—and repeat the process from January to December."[41]

The report went on to examine in some depth the various components of educational radio and celebrate their successes. Unlike the Top 40 noise machines, the authors asserted, educational radio was covering the hip and happening Now issues: "poverty, minorities, pollution, urban affairs, youth and student unrest, the new morality, and various social ills." For instance, WAMU Washington broadcast a conference on housing, work, transportation, and leisure featuring Vice President Hubert Humphrey, New York City Mayor John Lindsay, Vermont Governor Philip Hoff, and economist John Kenneth Galbraith.[42] The authors revealed the chronic blind spot of their kind when they failed to mention that this quartet of liberal Democrats was largely in agreement on the issues discussed; dissenting voices, whether conservative, libertarian, or New Left, were absent. The "issues" discussed in these venues came straight from the agenda of 1960s left-liberalism: the Great

Society was examined on WAER in Syracuse, New York; the Population Explosion on Washington's WAMU; Pornography on WBFO in Buffalo.[43]

Almost the only program straying from the stereotype was a series on Detroit's WDET focusing on six ethnic groups in the Motor City: Armenians, Croatians, Germans, Hungarians, Italians, and Poles.[44] These and other working-class white ethnic groups have historically been unheard and invisible on American public radio and television. Despite this blind spot, however, stations in such far-flung locales as Corvallis, Oregon; Manhattan, Kansas; Morehead, Kentucky; and Iowa City, Iowa, were, in sundry ways, able to treat local news at greater length and in greater depth than many of their commercial counterparts.

In-school educational radio, which has since gone the way of the Hula Hoop and drivers' ed filmstrips, was claimed by the authors to reach an audience of five to ten million children, a figure perhaps concocted by adding generous percentages of the school populations of such burgs as New York City, Cleveland, Chicago, St. Louis, and others whose school systems maintained stations. (For instance, the Land report cited a claim that 1.986 million children in and around Cleveland had benefited from educational radio.[45]) Radio was said to be an especially suitable medium for reaching pre-literate children. It was also advertised as superior to television in some respects, as for instance in giving freer play to children's imaginations. The Wisconsin State Network found that when schoolchildren watched its "Let's Draw" program on television, they tended to simply mimic in their drawings what they had seen on the screen. But radio gave wider rein to their creative impulses.[46] In sum, Herman Land and associates concluded, educational radio was "underfinanced, understaffed, underequipped, underpromoted and underresearched."[47] A boost in financing was the key to ridding these words of their *under* prefixes.

Grandiloquent language was absent from the Land volume, unlike the Carnegie Commission report. There was no soaring rhetoric or ethereal rhodomontade about the glorious works to be created when artists and public servants enjoyed freedom, or no patriotic hymns to the cheerful willingness of Americans to pay any price, bear any burden, when it came to subsidizing media. "When the most important immediate need is an office typewriter—an actual case—talk of new horizons of radio service must appear visionary at best," the authors conceded.[48] But if money doesn't change everything, at least it could end the typewriter shortage in the offices of the nation's educational radio stations.

Taking the handoff from his hand-picked Carnegie Commission, President Johnson, on February 28, 1967, delivered a "Message on Education and Health" in which he recommended enactment of a Public Television Act of 1967, which would create a Corporation for Public Television, to be funded with $9 million in seed money in FY 1968, and boost federal funding of television and radio facility construction by more than threefold, to $10.5 million in FY 1968.[49] Jack Mitchell calls this "the last major initiative of the Great Society."[50] (President Johnson was not exactly a disinterested observer: his fortune had been accumulated through the television and radio stations he and his wife, Lady Bird, had obtained through political favoritism by the FCC.)[51]

This seed money was supposed to bloom into a permanent funding source outside the annual congressional appropriations process, though it never did. The Carnegie Commission's recommended tax on TV sets was a non-starter, as were suggestions for a tax on the sale of radios and dedicated fees from commercial broadcasters for the use of satellite systems. The President's advisers halted the excise tax on televisions, which John Burke said "had never really been very popular with anyone."[52] It was, Johnson's aides pointed out, regressive and would hit hardest the poor, who—despite the earnest assurances of foundation types—had the least interest in the development of such a system. Bill Moyers, the LBJ press secretary and later eminence grise of PBS, tells another story. He claims that President Johnson applied the full-court press to win the excise tax, but House Ways and Means Committee Chairman Wilbur Mills (D-AR) pushed back, telling Johnson, "Well, that's all well and good, Lyndon. But you were up there long enough [in Congress] to know we ain't gonna give money to folks without some strings attached. We don't work that way."[53] Whether this episode of Mills the hard-headed deal-maker laying down the law to the idealistic Johnson happened just this way is up to each reader to decide. Doubts are understandable.

The excise tax, whether on radios or televisions or what have you, would have given public broadcasting a dedicated source of revenue removed from the direct control of congressional appropriators. The Ford Foundation's Fred Friendly, formerly president of CBS News, believed this to be an absolute necessity to safe-guard the integrity and independence of public broadcasting. But as Wilbur Mills allegedly told President Johnson, strings are *always* attached.

The President, never known for taking a hands-off approach to anything, insisted that public broadcasting "must be absolutely free from any federal government inter-ference over programming," and in the next paragraph of his message he called for the CPT's board of directors to consist of 15 members chosen by the President and confirmed by the Senate, thus ensuring that this entity would be a partisan tool from the cradle to its (not yet envisioned) grave.[54]

The legislative initiative which melded the President's recommendations with those of the Carnegie Commission had been drafted within the U.S. Department of Health, Education, and Welfare. Its Senate sponsor was Warren Magnuson, the Democrat from Washington State who was not-so-affectionately known as the Senator from Boeing, in recognition of the water-carrying he had done for his state's aviation and defense industries. Senator Magnuson's bill authorized the creation of a Public Corporation for Educational or Public Television. Radio was yet to appear on the radar screen of the relevant policymakers, though it was contemplated that the federal government would assist in the construction and maintenance of educational radio stations.

Congressional testimony was nearly unanimous in favor of the bill. Although radio was glaringly absent from the CPT's name, National Educational Radio's Jerrold Sandler spoke to the instructional potential of radio, the forgotten medium, and his remarks so impressed Senator Robert Griffin (R-MI) that the senator said to him, "I notice that under Title II the bill provides for the establishment of a corporation for public television. And yet as I understand the purpose and the function of this partic-ular corporation they are supposed to concern themselves with educational radio as well as television. Wouldn't you at least agree with me that the name of the corporation ought to be changed"—perhaps to the "corporation for public broadcasting"? Sandler, seemingly nonplussed, agreed that "that would be an excellent one," and the name was changed.[55]

But this was no accident, no providential coincidence. The backstory, as Jack Mitchell and Jerrold Sandler relate, was rooted in Senator Griffin's home state of Michigan and the University of Michigan's educational radio station WUOM, the cradle that rocked Mitchell, Sandler, and NAEB chairman Ed Burrows. Theirs was a "guerilla operation" which Mitchell, in retrospect, characterized as "a stealth strategy that involved misrepresentation, temper tantrums, and an inside connection in the Johnson administration." It was "anything but noble"—but it worked. It was Ed Burrows who engineered the hiring of Sandler, who had served as WUOM's program director, to serve as "what amounted to a radio lobbyist at the NAEB office in Washington."[56] At NAEB's headquarters, Sandler pled with his opposite number in the educational television division, Scott Fletcher, to advocate for the changing of the proposed Corporation for Public Television to the radio-inclusive Corporation for Public Broadcasting. Fletcher demurred. Educational TV was in no mood to split the anticipated federal pie. Radio could fend for itself.

Radio *did* fend for itself. There was more than one avenue of access to those who write the laws. Another WUOM alumnus, former chief engineer Dean Costen, was the deputy undersecretary of the Department of Health, Education, and Welfare, and at the prompting of his erstwhile comrades Sandler and Burrows, Costen inserted the words "and radio" wherever the word "television" appeared in the Johnson administration's draft legislation.

As Jack Mitchell explains, the educational television cognoscenti flipped out. They got to their people within HEW on the weekend before the administration was to send the bill to the Hill and had "and radio" removed. But friendly sources tipped off Sandler, who tipped off Costen, and by Monday morning "and radio" had been restored. The battle was on. Sandler, acting as the field general, deployed ground troops from around the country, the men and women who put educational radio on the air, to lobby their elected representatives. They succeeded; radio stayed.

The National Association of Educational Broadcasters, its television and radio divisions, agreed to support the "and radio" language. But the TV people, who believed they held the upper hand, insisted upon retaining the name Corporation for Public Television. They hadn't counted on the Michigan connection, however, and by Jack Mitchell's account, Ed Burrows planted a seed with Senator Griffin's staff that flowered into the colloquy in the committee room and which led, ultimately, to the nomenclatorial alteration to the Corporation for Public Broadcasting.[57]

Sandler, Burrows, and their allies who had inserted the "and radio" phrase would pay for their effrontery professionally. As Mitchell writes, "Their improbable victory also cost the small band of insurgents any role in public radio's future. They offended the very people who would run public broadcasting, people who were angered by the defeat and, more importantly, the less-than-honorable way it was achieved. None of those who went to battle for radio earned leadership roles in the new public radio system that emerged from their efforts."[58]

(Jack Mitchell himself is a central and thoughtful figure in the public radio story. This product of WUOM, the University of Michigan's radio station, holds the distinction of being National Public Radio's first employee. The CPB picked him up from this farm team and sent him to England for further seasoning at the BBC before recalling him to the States, where on August 15, 1970, he went to work at 888 16th Street, NW, in Washington, DC, CPB's headquarters. He would, as he explains in his book on the culture of NPR, write the institution's first strategic plan, helm its first newscast, and serve as the first "permanent [*sic*] producer" of *All Things Considered*.[59] He would leave DC in 1976 to spend the bulk of his career with Wisconsin Public Radio, though he was named chairman of the board of directors of NPR in 1985.)

The legislation made the journey from conception to development to passage with "astonishing smoothness."[60] The Magnuson bill was approved by the full Senate by voice vote. The most significant amendment at the committee level provided that six of the fifteen CPB members would be chosen by the other nine members rather than by the President—a pinprick against the Imperial Presidency that was removed during the House-Senate conference. (Currently, the CPB board consists of nine members, of which not more than five may be members of one political party. The President nominates all nine, subject to confirmation by the Senate. The staggered terms are six years in length.)

Despite the voice vote approval, there were scattered voices of dissent in the Senate. South Carolina's Strom Thurmond, a former Democrat who had recently crossed party lines into the GOP, said that "nothing in this bill safeguards against the capture of the corporation by a small clique with definite ideological biases."[61] He was not referring to Dixiecrats.

The House version was introduced by Rep. Harley O. Staggers (D-WV), chairman of the Committee on Interstate and Foreign Commerce. Curiously, the largest grant in the history of the ETV Facilities Act of 1962 was made to WWVU in Morgantown, West Virginia, just one week before hearings began in Rep. Staggers's committee.[62] Surely this was just coincidence!

Unlike in the Senate, critics of the legislation were vocal in the House. These tended to be "Southern Democrats and conservative Republicans." Their concerns were the expense and, for some, the potential of federal interference in an ostensibly free medium. Others complained that instructional television had been slighted. However, the 80 witnesses before the House Committee on Interstate and Foreign Commerce included just one opponent of the public television bill, the unprepossessing Leonard B. Stevens of the All-Channel Television Society, who spoke in defense of the independent UHF stations which would face competition from the bulked-up public stations.[63]

Somewhat hyperbolically, conservative spokesman Rep. Samuel Devine (R-OH) asserted that the American "economic system is on the verge of collapse and many desirable things must be put aside indefinitely. Could anyone seriously argue that this program to enhance public broadcasting is indispensable?"[64] Indispensable, perhaps not, but advocates saw in it the possibility of a general intellectual and social uplift.

Supporters reassured skeptics that a national government-run network was not contemplated by this bill; it would be, rather, a system of interconnected stations which could draw on productions from other public stations or the national production facilities, but control and a good deal of programming would remain local. The Corporation for Public Broadcasting would own no stations, operate no stations, and endorse no political candidates. Should CPB cross that line, cautioned Senator Norris Cotton (R-NH), the congressional appropriations committees would pull the plug on its funding.[65] To ensure against this, Rep. William Lee Springer (R-IL) succeeded in adding an amendment prohibiting "editorializing" by any "noncommercial educational broadcasting station."[66] (This ban would eventually be gutted by the U.S. Supreme Court in *Federal Communications Commission v. League of Women Voters of California* (1984), in which a divided Court ruled by a 5–4 margin that the prohibition on editorializing violated the First Amendment.[67])

The bill encountered unexpected, if temporary, opposition on the House floor. A motion to recommit the bill to the committee failed by only 194–167, after which the bill was passed by a vote of 266–81 with one member voting present.[68] A conference committee reconciled the relatively minor differences between the Senate and House bills, each body approved the conference report, and President Johnson signed into law the Public Broadcasting Act of 1967 on November 7, 1967.

Johnson's remarks upon the signing asserted that "the purpose of this act" is to "enrich man's spirit." He largely ignored radio, the afterthought of the act, and instead expressed the hope that "public television would help make our Nation a replica of the old Greek marketplace, where public affairs took place in view of all the citizens."[69] Coming from a president whose administration included such shielded or mendacious acts as the Gulf of Tonkin and the wiretapping of numerous American citizens, this was a bit rich, but speechwriters must be served.

Title I of the Public Broadcasting Act of 1967 built on the Educational Facilities Act of 1962, providing for federal aid in the construction of "educational television broadcasting facilities" and "noncommercial educational radio broadcasting facilities."[70]

Title II was the meat of the act. It created a Corporation for Public Broadcasting, whose 15-person board was appointed by the President with the approval of the Senate. These fifteen were to represent, "as nearly as practicable"—a loophole through which one could drive a tank—the "various regions of the country, various professions and occupations, and various kinds of talent and experience appropriate to the functions and responsibilities of the Corporation." Despite the rhetorical nod toward inclusivity, farmers, truck drivers, housewives, clerical workers, punk rockers, Tennessee hair-braiders, Idaho homeschoolers, and Allentown police officers have been conspicuous by their absence from the CPB board. The President and Senate were also instructed that "no political test or qualification shall be used in selecting, appointing, promoting, or taking other personnel actions with respect to officers, agents, and employees of the Corporation," but members of the many partisan challengers to the Republican and Democratic duopoly—the American Independent, Peoples', Socialist Workers, Libertarian, Citizens, Constitution, Reform, and Green parties, among others—have yet to be appointed to this ostensibly nonpartisan (read: *bi*partisan) board.[71]

The CPB was charged with "channeling"—an apt verb—funds ($9 million in the fiscal year 1968) "for use by noncommercial television and radio production groups, to stimulate programming of higher education and cultural value through financial aid and recommendations to local stations and educational TV networks, and to arrange for systems of regional interconnection to extend educational broadcasting's audience." The CPB was barred from owning or operating television or radio stations, systems, or networks, which in theory was a safeguard against excessive centralization. Programs eligible for CPB subsidy were those "primarily designed for educational or cultural purposes." (A House addendum reading "and not primarily for amusement or entertainment purposes" was dropped in conference, thus protecting several decades' worth of Peter, Paul, and Mary specials.)[72]Congressional concern over the propaganda potential of a federally subsidized media empire gave rise to the edict under the "purposes and activities" subsection that public broadcasters will observe "strict adherence to objectivity and balance in all programs or series of programs of a controversial nature."[73]

That remained to be seen.

Notes of Chapter

1.   Burke, *An Historical-Analytical Study of the Legislative and Political Origins of the Public Broadcasting Act of 1967*, p. 88.
2.   Ibid., p. 93.
3.   *Public Television: A Program for Action; A Report of the Carnegie Commission on Educational Television* (New York: Bantam, 1967), p. viii.
4.   Ibid., p. vii.
5.   Burke, *An Historical-Analytical Study of the Legislative and Political Origins of the Public Broadcasting Act of 1967*, p. 105.
6.   *Public Television: A Program for Action; A Report of the Carnegie Commission on Educational Television*, pp. viii-ix.
7.   "E.B. White's Letter to the First Carnegie Commission," September 26, 1966, *Current*, www.current.org, accessed September 12, 2019.
8.   Trevor Burrus, "Big Bird's Fuzzy Defenders March on Washington," *USA Today*, October 31, 2012.
9.   *Public Television: A Program for Action; A Report of the Carnegie Commission on Educational Television*, p. 92.
10. James Ledbetter, *Made Possible By....The Death of Public Broadcasting in the United States* (New York: Verso/1997/1998), p. 45.
11. Ibid., p. 46.
12. Ibid., pp. 45, 61.
13. *Public Television: A Program for Action; A Report of the Carnegie Commission on Educational Television*, p. 4.
14. President Lyndon B. Johnson, "State of the Union Address," January 10, 1967, https://millercenter.org/the-presidency/presidential-speeches/january-10-1967-state-union-address.

15. *Public Television: A Program for Action; A Report of the Carnegie Commission on Educational Television*, p. 3.
16. Ibid., pp. 4–9.
17. Ibid., p. 42.
18. Ibid., pp. 69–70.
19. David Sarnoff, "Uncensored and Uncontrolled," *The Nation* (July 23, 1924): 90.
20. Mary S. Mander, "The Public Debate about Broadcasting in the Twenties: An Interpretive History," *Journal of Broadcasting*, Vol. 28, No. 2 (Spring 1984): 180.
21. *Public Television: A Program for Action; A Report of the Carnegie Commission on Educational Television*, pp. 8–9.
22. Ibid., p. 80.
23. Ibid., p. 87.
24. Ibid., p. 37.
25. Ibid., p. 69.
26. Ibid., pp. 98–99.
27. "A Public Trust: Report of the second Carnegie Commission," April 3, 1979, *Current*, www.current.org, accessed January 13, 2020.
28. Sandler, Introduction, *The Hidden Medium: A Status Report on Educational Radio in the United States*, p. iv.
29. Ibid., p. v.
30. Ibid., p. i.
31. Herman W. Land Associates, *The Hidden Medium: A Status Report on Educational Radio in the United States*, p. I-1.
32. Ibid., p. I-3.
33. Ibid., p. I-22. Typically, such programs were broadcast by university-related stations, for instance, those attached to Oregon State, Washington State, and the universities of Iowa and Florida.
34. Ibid., pp. I-1–2.
35. Ibid., pp. I-3–4.
36. Ibid., p. I-4.
37. Ibid., p. I-5.
38. Ibid., p. I-8.
39. Fourteen managers of 10-W stations reported being adequately staffed, fourteen reported being understaffed, and two did not answer the question. Ibid., p. I-9.
40. Ibid., p. I-13.
41. Ibid., p. II-42.
42. Ibid., pp. II-2–4.
43. Ibid., p. II-23.
44. Ibid., p. II-5.
45. Ibid., p. II-30.
46. Ibid., p. II-35.
47. Ibid., p. I-28.

48. Ibid.
49. Burke, *An Historical-Analytical Study of the Legislative and Political Origins of the Public Broadcasting Act of 1967*, p. 148.
50. Mitchell, *Listener Supported: The Culture and History of Public Radio*, p. 29.
51. Jack Shafer, "The Honest Graft of Lady Bird Johnson," *Slate*, July 16, 2007, www.slate.com. See also Robert A. Caro, *The Years of Lyndon Johnson: Means of Ascent* (New York: Knopf, 1990).
52. Burke, *An Historical-Analytical Study of the Legislative and Political Origins of the Public Broadcasting Act of 1967*, p. 119.
53. Bill Moyers, "Wilbur Mills to LBJ: 'We ain't gonna give money to folks without some strings attached,' " *Current*, www.current.org, May 18, 2006.
54. Burke, *An Historical-Analytical Study of the Legislative and Political Origins of the Public Broadcasting Act of 1967*, p. 148.
55. Ibid., pp. 183–84.
56. Mitchell, *Listener Supported: The Culture and History of Public Radio*, p. 34.
57. Ibid., p. 41. Noah Adams, who cohosted *All Things Considered* between 1982 and 2002, with an interruption, wrote in his history of the early years of NPR, "'And radio.'….Very late on a winter night in 1967, those words were typed repeatedly, then cut out with scissors and Scotch-taped onto the pages of the Public Television bill that was about to leave the White House and be introduced in Congress. At the last minute, the draft language for the lawmakers was changed to insert 'and radio' after every significant mention of television." Well, sort of. Adams also dismisses the pre-NPR world of educational radio stations as "part-time, poorly funded, and attracting few listeners." Noah Adams, "And Radio," *This is NPR: The First Forty Years* (San Francisco: Chronicle Books, 2010), p. 21.
58. Mitchell, *Listener Supported: The Culture and History of Public Radio*, p. 41.
59. Ibid., p. x.
60. Barnouw, *Tube of Plenty: The Evolution of American Television*, p. 398.
61. Chase, "Public Broadcasting and the Problem of Government Influence: Towards a Legislative Solution," *University of Michigan Journal of Law Reform*: 74.
62. Burke, *An Historical-Analytical Study of the Legislative and Political Origins of the Public Broadcasting Act of 1967*, p. 195.
63. Ibid., pp. 197, 202.
64. Huntsberger, "Attempting an Affirmation Approach to American Broadcasting: Ideology, Politics, and the Public Telecommunications Facilities Program," *Journalism & Mass Communication Quarterly*: 767.
65. Mike Gonzalez, "Is There Any Justification for Continuing to Ask Taxpayers to Fund NPR and PBS?" Knight Foundation, December 7, 2017, www.knightfoundation.org.
66. Burke, *An Historical-Analytical Study of the Legislative and Political Origins of the Public Broadcasting Act of 1967*, p. 208.
67. David Schultz, "*Federal Communications Commission v. League of Women Voters of California*," The First Amendment Encyclopedia, https://www.mtsu.

edu/first-amendment/article/110/federal-communications-commission-v-lea gue-of-women-voters-of-california, accessed September 17, 2019.

68. Burke, *An Historical-Analytical Study of the Legislative and Political Origins of the Public Broadcasting Act of 1967*, p. 217.

69. "President Johnson's Remarks," November 7, 1967, CPB, https://www.cpb. org/aboutpb/act/remarks.

70. Public Law 90–129, November 7, 1967, Title 1.

71. Public Law 90–129, November 7, 1967, Title II.

72. Ibid. Chase, "Public Broadcasting and the Problem of Government Influence: Towards a Legislative Solution," *University of Michigan Journal of Law Reform*: 70.

73. Public Law 90–129, November 7, 1967, Title II.

Chapter 5
Washington Versus The Sticks

Broadcasting historian Erik Barnouw, author of *Tube of Plenty: The Evolution of American Television* (1976), cites President Johnson's obsessions with Vietnam and domestic dissent as a crucial contributing cause to the creation of the Corporation for Public Broadcasting. He notes that Johnson handpicked as the corporation's first chairman Frank Pace, Jr., who had served as both Secretary of the Army and chief executive officer of General Dynamics—"an embodiment of the military-industrial complex." Pace had, according to Barnouw, "commissioned research on… how public television might be used for riot control."[1]

Pace envisioned the CPB as a "gradually growing social asset that could add to the nation's awareness of the democracy's strengths and resources in information and the arts." Okay, he wasn't much of a prose stylist, but his 15-member board was, as Senator Warren Magnuson (D-WA) gushed, "One of the finest groups of Americans ever put together on one board."[2] In addition to Pace, they included Robert S. Benjamin, an attorney and chairman of United Artists; former LBJ aide Jack J. Valenti, president of the Motion Picture Association of America and speaker of the immortal lines, "I sleep better at night knowing Lyndon Johnson is President"; Milton S. Eisenhower, presidential brother and former president of Johns Hopkins University; James R. Killian Jr., chairman of the Carnegie Commission; Joseph A. Bierne, president of the Communications Workers of America; Michael A. Gammino, a Providence, RI, bank president; Oveta Culp Hobby, chair of the board of the *Houston Post*; Joseph D. Hughes, a prominent figure in the constellation of Mellon family interests; former Georgia Governor Carl E. Sanders; prominent insurance company attorney Roscoe C. Carroll; Saul Haas, chairman of the TV-radio stations KIRO in Seattle; Erich Leinsdorf, music director of the Boston Symphony Orchestra, Frank E. Schooley, director of broadcasting at the University of Illinois; and John D. Rockefeller III of the Rockefeller Fund.[3] If they were not artists, they certainly knew where to locate the money that might support artists.

To cover the gap between the passage of the Public Broadcasting Act of 1967 and the distribution of funds, the Ford Foundation awarded $20 million in grants to National Educational Television, the Children's Television Workshop, and other

© The Author(s), under exclusive license to Springer Nature Switzerland AG 2021
J. T. Bennett, *The History and Politics of Public Radio*, Studies in Public Choice 41,
https://doi.org/10.1007/978-3-030-80019-2_5

entities which were expected to be major players in the expanding world of public broadcasting, though as George H. Gibson writes in his history of federal involvement in public broadcasting, "There was some grumbling that the money would have been better spent by distributing it to stations to make their own decisions at the grass roots level rather than to those national organizations and through the centralized procedures."[4] The tug of war between the centralizers and decentralizers was just beginning. The federal role was purported by supporters to be modest, though as is typically the case when the federal government begins to subsidize a state, local, or private activity, Washington's role expanded apace. Louisiana Democratic Rep. John Rarick, who held down the rightmost flank of his party, called the CPB "a runaway brainwashing monster," staking out the outer limits of criticism in 1968.[5] But there was confusion about just how these federal funds were supposed to be used.

Thanks to the Michigan educational radio mafia, the words "and radio" and "broadcasting" had ensured a role for the federal government in the next evolutionary step for educational radio. But what would that step be? Fully 86% of Americans had access to public radio—but how to persuade them to listen?[6] A New England public TV pioneer with the evocative name of Hartford Gunn had one idea. Gunn, who embodied what Jack Mitchell called a "Bostonian's contempt for those Midwest land-grant state university stations at the heart of educational radio," suggested that what he termed a National Public Radio System be centered in a handful of coastal metropolitan stations, which would produce programs to be heard over the nation-wide network.[7] Headquartered in Washington DC, the national staff would produce "tightly-formatted, in-depth national and international news and public affairs, with the emphasis on analysis, commentary, criticism, and good talk," the last feature presumably in cultivated accents.[8] Gunn, who later went on to helm PBS, misfired, for those Midwesterners who were the target of his patronizing solicitude "would never turn over their enterprise to the arrogant gentleman from Boston."[9]

On a likelier track, Samuel C.O. Holt, a product of Princeton and a Rhodes Scholarship who had launched the first all-news radio station in the South in Birmingham, Alabama, published in 1969 the *Public Radio Study*, a CPB- and Ford Foundation-funded report proposing the broad outlines of what became National Public Radio, to be embedded in a Radio Division of the Corporation for Public Broadcasting.

Only "more money can solve the financial problems" of educational radio, the Holt report stated somewhat obviously, recommending that such support be given by both the CPB and the Ford Foundation.[10] The involvement of the Ford Foundation, Rockefeller family charities, and other bigfoot foundations provokes a rude question: Was their advocacy of federally funded public broadcasting a clever if disingenuous way of transferring the burden of sponsoring such ventures from them to the taxpayers? As the avant-garde literary critic Richard Kostelanetz impudently noted, "public funding of large arts institutions [has] taken private philanthropy off its increasingly expensive hook."[11] The Rockefeller charities had been especially energetic supporters of the creation of the National Endowment for the Arts, which provided sizeable grants to museums whose underwriting had long been the province of foundations endowed by the exceptionally wealthy. Similarly, the Ford Foundation was active in its support of a federal role for educational broadcasting, which had been part of Ford's philanthropic portfolio.

Meanwhile, educational radio stations were abuzz over the prospect of a pot of federal money opening up to them. Representatives of the 425-station-member National Educational Radio Division of the National Association of Educational Broadcasters convened in Madison, Wisconsin, in August 1969, and out of their meeting came a recommendation that the CPB fulfill its assigned mission to "encourage the growth and development of public radio" by creating something called National Public Radio.[12] The NAEB's Radio Division, betraying a charming naïveté in the ways of Washington DC, suggested that National Public Radio be governed by a 12-person board whose hallmark would be geographic diversity: one member each would hail from the nine regions into which the NAEB had divided the country, and the other three would be members of the public elected by these nine.[13] There was, of course, no way in the ether that the powers-that-be of public broadcasting were going to cede control of this newly created fiefdom to people from places like Idaho, New Mexico, and Mississippi.

National Public Radio was incorporated in March of 1970, but it would not go on the air until over a year later, on April Fool's Day, 1971, when it was carried over 90 stations in 32 states. Although there were 457 FCC-licensed educational radio stations in the United States, typically affiliated with high schools, colleges, and universities, most lacked the power and the hours to make them eligible to affiliate with NPR.[14] Eighty-three percent of the new NPR affiliates broadcast on FM.[15]

Eligibility for CPB funds depended upon a station's meeting minimum standards for broadcast hours (in 1970, 8 h daily, 6 days weekly, and 48 weeks yearly) and paid staff (one full-time, four half-time). As Ralph Engelman notes in his history of public radio and television in America, only 73 educational stations, or 17% of the total number, met those standards in 1970.[16] To grass-roots non-profit radio stalwarts, these bars seemed designed to punish the little guys while rewarding the bigger ones: a classic example of the (relatively) rich getting richer, and an ominous sign that federally sponsored radio would be influenced disproportionately by the larger cities and the *Ins* as opposed to the *Outs*.

"National Public Radio Purposes," which Jack Mitchell describes as the institution's "founding document," was the product of Bill Siemering, foremost among the founding spirits of NPR.[17] Bill Siemering was born to this, it would seem. He grew up "within sight of the WHA towers," whence originated the signal of the Madison, Wisconsin, station that laid claim to being the first whose offerings were intended for public consumption. As a student at UW, he was a jack of all trades at WHA, and in 1962 he took over WBFO, the University of Buffalo-affiliated station, with the aim of infusing some of the WHA spirit into the Queen City.

Siemering was a man of his time. "The airwaves belong to the people," he declared, and it wasn't just hot air.[18] WBFO set up a studio in the ghetto and produced a series of programs aimed at Buffalo's African American population, including the quaintly titled "To Be a Negro."[19] WBFO covered Vietnam protests on campus and sought to air various viewpoints, for as Siemering said, in words redolent of the hippie era, truth is "reflected through different perceptions of reality, and we broadcast a full spectrum of opinion."[20] His commitment to letting listeners hear an abundance of voices and views was akin to the philosophy of Pacifica founder Lewis Hill, if not the NPR of Terry Gross and Co.

"National Public Radio Purposes" was a mission statement of sorts, before those seemingly obligatory sentence-clots became nothing but formula and base-touching. Siemering waxed exuberant: "National Public Radio will serve the individual; it will promote personal growth; it will regard the individual differences among men with respect and joy rather than derision and hate; it will celebrate the human experience as infinitely varied rather than vacuous and banal; it will encourage a sense of active constructive participation, rather than apathetic helplessness."

That has a distinctly '60–'70s feel to it, something of a cross between the New Left's humanistic Port Huron Statement and an earnest self-help tome of the Me Decade, but it also has life and passion and conviction and excitement behind it. Even a curmudgeon, a skeptic of the value and legitimacy of federal support of radio, might nod in agreement with Siemering's optimistic pledge: "In its cultural mode, National Public Radio will preserve and transmit the cultural past [and] will encourage and broadcast the work of contemporary artists." This promised not only music spanning the range from Beethoven to Bernstein but poets from Dickinson to Ginsberg, dramatists from Shakespeare to Albee, story tellers from Hawthorne to Bellow.

The mission statement tiptoed to the edge of political engagement: "In its journalistic mode, National Public Radio will actively explore, investigate and interpret issues of national and international import. The programs will enable the individual to better understand himself, his government, his institutions, and his natural and social environment so he can intelligently participate in effecting the process of change."[21] That last word is, as mission statement writers of the twenty-first century might say, *problematic*. Change is a loaded word embedded in the lexicon of progressivism. It is the antithesis of *conservation*, which the intelligent citizen might also undertake, and it forecloses *renewal*, another option left off the mission statement table. It is, to use the political imagery of the era, a Hubert Humphrey word, a Nelson Rockefeller word, a Birch Bayh word, and not one common in the vocabulary of Barry Goldwater, Gerald Ford, or Sam Ervin.

Compare and contrast NPR's current mission statement, which might have been designed by an automaton in any college or university human relations department in our age when no modern entity is truly alive until it disgorges a mission statement...

The mission of NPR is to work in partnership with member stations to create a more informed public—one challenged and invigorated by a deeper understanding and appreciation of events, ideas, and cultures. To accomplish our mission, we produce, acquire, and distribute programming that meets the highest standards of public service in journalism and cultural expression; we represent our members in matters of their mutual interest; and we provide satellite interconnection for the entire public radio system.[22]

... with Simering's ringing conclusion to his mission statement:

The total service should be trustworthy, enhance intellectual development, expand knowledge, deepen aural esthetic enjoyment, increase the pleasure of living in a pluralistic society and result in a service to listeners which makes them more responsive, informed human beings and intelligent responsible citizens of their communities and the world.

That sounded like a goal worth pursuing, even if reasonable men and women might disagree on the proper method of its financing. Once it got down to cases, Siemering's "National Public Radio Purposes" exited its lofty plane and entered the world of the practical. Its core priorities were:

1. "Provide an identifiable daily product which is consistent and reflects the highest standards of broadcast journalism."

This did not mean aping CBS News or installing a Harry Reasoner epigone as the chief newsreader. "Hard news," while not ignored, would take a back seat to "interpretation, investigative reporting on public affairs, the world of ideas and the arts." As if to distinguish this set of tasks from those performed by the light-feature reporters or think-piece pontificators of the mainstream media, Siemering declares that National Public Radio will not "substitute superficial blandness for genuine diversity of regions, values, and cultural and ethnic minorities which comprise American society; it would speak with many voices and many dialects." Wyoming cowboys, Oklahoma ranchers, Alabama bluesmen, Cape Cod eccentrics.... all would have a voice on this exciting new broadcast venture. Poets, scholars, farmers, and regular folk would find a home over its airwaves.

This vision is separated by a Grand Canyonesque chasm from the eventual reality of the sexless, accentless NPR male voice and the upper-middle-class, private-college-educated female voice that came to dominate especially the Washington-produced staples of the system. As we shall see, a great preponderance of stories on NPR are focused on the elite precincts of the northeast, the spindly coastal archipelago connecting Washington with New York City with Boston. Those Wyoming cowboys and Alabama bluesmen are exotic outliers in that universe.

Siemering also insisted that "National Public Radio will not regard its audience as a 'market' or in terms of its disposable income"—easy to do if revenue is not one of your major concerns, as Uncle Sam is paying the bills. In this instance, too, the vision is sharply at odds with what came next, as NPR has boasted of and catered to its disposable-income-heavy listenership.

2. "Provide extended coverage of public events, issues and ideas, and acquire, and produce special public affairs programs."

In this regard, Siemering anticipated C-SPAN, the cable and satellite television network devoted to public-affairs programming, most prominently coverage of the U.S. Congress. Siemering envisioned not only the audio broadcast of congressional hearings but also of regulatory agencies—and here, admittedly, the prospect is raised of listeners falling into the deepest of sleeps—as well as NPR-sponsored debates on the issues of the day. (PBS, by contrast with NPR, is barred from producing programs for its member stations, though it distributes programs which have been produced by member stations with funds passed through from Washington.)

Again, however, Siemering crosses the line into an advocacy that sits uneasily with federal sponsorship. "National Public Radio," he writes, "through public affairs programs, would not only call attention to a problem but **be an active agent in seeking solutions** [emphasis added]." He instances the issue of minority hiring in the construction trades, something of a softball, as even in 1970 discriminatory union practices were frowned upon by all but those who directly benefitted from them, and they were clearly on the way out. Nevertheless, even with a rather clear-cut issue, the question remains: Ought a media outlet subsidized by federal taxpayers be advocating—taking sides—serving as an active agent in seeking solutions—in the matter of political debates or controversies?

3. "Acquire and produce cultural programs which can be scheduled individually by stations."

This is where Siemering let his imagination run wild, as he conjured up a series of ideas that would have showcased and explored the cultural riches of America—including yesterday's America, as he emphasized "an equal need to preserve and transmit the culture of the past." That few or none of these ideas ever became part of NPR's working reality was perhaps sealed as fate when Washington DC, became its nerve center. Specifically, this section of "National Public Radio Purposes" proposed to:

- Hold national competitions to encourage new writers for radio.
- Encourage "leading writers of fiction and dramatists" to write for radio.
- Engage in honest self-examination by "broadcasting regular criticisms of the medium."
- Commission writers of children's books to write for radio.
- Encourage local music scenes through national broadcasts: "Rather than a series of the New York Philharmonic, there could be a concert series with a different local orchestra each week performing what it does best."
- Highlight the music of the many ethnic groups that make up the American populace.

These suggestions put flesh on the bare-bones localism that NPR's founders sometimes spoke of. Though occasionally voices from the provinces have made themselves heard over public radio since 1970, these tend to say the same things, perhaps in slightly different accents and with a bit of vernacular idiosyncrasy thrown in for local color. As for trenchant criticism of the medium, including its public component, that is all but absent. Sure, one heard, in his heyday, slighting references to Rush Limbaugh, but any sharp critique of NPR itself would be written off as right-wing polemics, or the fevered dreams of paranoids from the swamps.

4. "Provide access to the intellectual and cultural resources of cities, universities, and rural districts through a system of cooperative program development with member public radio stations."

Again, building on this envisioned model would have provided a solid base for localism. Siemering explained that "each member station will have the potential of being an originator of programs as well as a transmitter; it will be national in input as well as distribution."

Certainly, stations such as Boston's WBUR-FM have originated programming, but overwhelmingly this has not been the case for NPR outlets in the Missoula, Montanas, the Topeka, Kansases, the Columbia, South Carolinas, and the Amarillo, Texases, across the fruited plain. They are passive receptors and transmitters of programs produced in the nation's largest metropoles by people largely of similar—that, is non-Missoulan, non-Topekan, non-Columbian, non-Amarilloan—background.

5. "Develop and distribute programs to specific groups (adult education, instructional, modular units for local productions) which meet needs of individual regions or groups."

Siemering channeled his inner 1950s sociologist in describing this priority: "As man pulls himself out of the mass society to develop his unique humanness, his minority identification (ethnic, cultural, value) becomes increasingly important."[23] Frank Mankiewicz, the McGovern campaign official who later became NPR president, complained that this goal had become realized all too well. He bemoaned the "snail-darter" mentality that he believed over-emphasized minorities at the expense of our commonality.

Bill Siemering was named the new organization's director of programming, but he lasted just two years before being canned by NPR president Don Quayle (no apparent relation to President George H. W. Bush's risible vice president) in December 1972, a dubious Christmas present. Siemering is said by some old hands to have been a poor personnel manager: an idea man, not an efficient get-things-done type like Quayle. The former had a looser, shaggier conception of public radio, shorn of pomposity, Eastern prep-school accents, and smooth professionalism; the latter seems to have conceived of the nascent institution as a more elevated iteration of the establishment media, backed by a classical soundtrack. The straitlaced Quayle, a Utah native who later became general manager of WGBH in Boston and one of the early mandarins of post-World War II educational radio, was more a manager than a visionary.[24] (Weep not for Siemering, whose later accomplishments included winning a MacArthur Foundation fellowship and mentoring "independent" radio in the less developed world.)

Siemering's final and lasting gift to NPR was *All Things Considered*, a daily 90-min magazine of the air which would not limit itself to carrying the practiced observations of "coolly objective journalists," said Siemering, but instead be closer to a Whitmanesque cacophony of diverse American voices.[25] *All Things Considered* gave NPR a chance to get the jump on the television and radio networks, whose primary daily news coverage was typically at 6:00 or 6:30 pm. Beamed out to 90 stations at first, today it is heard over ten times as many stations and airs live from 4:00 pm to 6:00 Eastern time. *All Things Considered*, or *ATC*, was distinguished in its early years, according to Joseph P. Duggan, then a young conservative observer, later a speechwriter for President George H. W. Bush, by a blend of "countercultural cheekiness and liberal piety," with plenty of reporters interviewing other reporters mixed in.[26] But it had a human, often quirky or endearing side. Susan Stamberg,

ATC cohost from 1972 to 1986, insisted that her commitment to her family dictated an abbreviated work schedule, and her bosses assented.

Bill Siemering laid down a simple law: "We're going to talk to our listeners just the way we talk to our friends."[27] He hated that "insufferable announcer sound."[28] Most of us, for better or worse, lack friends who speak in the de-sexed, accent-less, classic NPR cadence, with that hint, or more than a hint, of superciliousness, or perhaps just mild condescension, as if one were kindly imparting a bit of common knowledge to a friend whose powers of mentation were not quite up to snuff.

ATC launched May 3, 1971, the month after NPR went on the air, as its staff of five reporters waded out into a massive anti-Vietnam War demonstration in the nation's capital. It was a baptism of fire, and the green but enthusiastic staff pulled it off, despite a technical hitch or two. Bill Siemering explained that "[w]e wanted to capitalize on the sound quality of radio to tell stories, to escape from the sterility of a soundproof studio, and to give the listener a sense of being present amidst the action.... What followed was an extraordinary twenty-four-minute sound portrait of the events as they happened, with the voices of protesters, police, and office workers above the sirens and chopping of helicopters. Yes, there were flaws, and yet it stands as probably the best sound record of that historic day."[29] Although this baptism by fire occurred in the nation's capital, Siemering, in his brief tenure, envisioned a decentralized system which took its character and flavor from local stations; El Paso and St. Paul and Birmingham would be just as important to National Public Radio as were Washington and New York. Ordinary folk of the sort who don't seem to be what we consider public-radio types would be heard on these airwaves, or so the idealist out of Wisconsin by way of Buffalo dreamt. But Siemering was canned very early on, and his vision faded to black. Despite occasional lip service to decentralization, NPR's accent was distinctly Washington–New York–Boston.

Nixon V. The CPB

The public broadcasting infrastructure expanded rapidly, cultivated by government monies. HEW-administered facilities grants enabled dozens of new stations to start up, and others to expand. In 1974, 82% of the funding of public radio stations within the CPB system came from the government, with 54.6% derived from state and local governments and 27.4% from the federal government.[30] But the growth of PBS and NPR was concomitant with enhanced criticism. The Nixon administration, ever alert to the existence of enemies both real and imagined, took notice of public broadcasting's liberal bent—and acted.

Clay Whitehead, an electrical engineering Ph.D. from MIT and a Rand Corporation researcher who signed on with the Nixon campaign at the tender age of 29, headed the executive branch's Office of Telecommunication Policy, which President Nixon created on September 4, 1970, to replace the Office of Telecommunication Management. The office, which those in more glamorous postings may have considered a bit of a sleepy backwater, included two staffers who went on to distinguished careers: assistant to the director for media and congressional relations Brian P. Lamb, the presiding spirit of C-SPAN; and general counsel Antonin Scalia, a future U.S. Supreme Court justice.

George Gibson describes Whitehead as the "[Spiro] Agnew of public broadcasting," though conceding that he was "much brighter and more sophisticated" than Nixon's vice president, who served as the administration's point man for the culture war. Like Agnew, Whitehead could turn a phrase; he attacked network television news as a purveyor of "ideological plugola."[31] Yet Whitehead was more than an attack dog. He bemoaned the potential centralization of public broadcasting in Washington DC, warning, presciently, that news and public affairs programming will be "coordinated by people with similar outlooks."[32] To counter this DC groupthink—or, more cynically, to dilute the power of the anti-Nixon liberals who dominated the public broadcasting establishment—Whitehead and his confreres proposed "communications federalism," or the dispersion of funds and influence from Washington DC, to the provinces.[33]

The criticism of the CPB as overly centralized was not limited to Nixon partisans. Arthur L. Singer Jr., whose influence was critical in the formation of the Carnegie Commission, scored public broadcasting for departing from the "pluralism" and "localism" which he saw as embodied in the Carnegie report. "The present system is not pluralistic," he said as PBS was in its toddler stage. "It is dominated by the Corporation for Public Broadcasting, the Public Broadcasting Service and the Ford Foundation. What goes on the air on the system… is what these institutions approve."[34] Singer, a long-time administrator at the Massachusetts Institute of Technology and the Sloan Foundation, called PBS programming "every bit as centralized and in its own way as dehumanized as the network programming of CBS or NBC." Local stations, he said, had been reduced to "branch offices for Washington and New York."[35]

The U.S. Senate report on the Public Broadcasting Act of 1967 had insisted "in the strongest terms possible" that "local stations be absolutely free to determine for themselves what they should or should not broadcast….[L]ocal autonomy of stations and diversity of program sources will provide operational safeguards to assure the democratic functioning of the system."[36] A Washington-centric or -directed system ran diametrically opposed to the Senate's understanding—or ostensible understanding—of the act.

Nixon's pugnacious aide Patrick J. Buchanan saw the Corporation for Public Broadcasting as a nest of liberals who vainly sought to camouflage their bias with the "fig leaf" of William F. Buckley's television program *Firing Line*.[37] It was, in the conservative wordsmith's phrase, "an upholstered playpen for liberal broadcasters." (Buchanan says that Nixon, after leaving office, told him that he agreed with Buchanan that he should have "terminate[d] all federal funding."[38]) The Nixon White House refused to give NPR reporters White House press credentials, an act of pettiness not likely to have improved the fledgling news organization's coverage of the president. In fairness, though, Jack Mitchell writes, "With the possible exception of a few engineers, NPR's staff, to a person, disliked Nixon and hated the war he failed to end."[39]

In 1969, when the Corporation for Public Broadcasting was up for reauthorization, the outgoing Johnson administration had requested a five-year extension of the authorization, with an FY 1970 authorization of $20 million, or a fourfold increase from FY 1969. The new Nixon administration halved that to $10 million—still a doubling of funds for the CPB. Robert Finch, Nixon's Secretary of Health, Education, and Welfare, suggested that all involved should figure out a way "to encourage private enterprise to contribute" as well.[40] The Democratic Congress negated this effort and sent the president legislation providing for a one-year reauthorization at $20 million, and Nixon signed it.[41]

Three years later, however, and more or less coincident with the Watergate affair, Nixon vetoed the bill providing funding for the Corporation for Public Broadcasting on June 30, 1972. The President's veto message emphasized the Whitehead critique, claiming that the "most serious and widespread concern" about the CPB was "that an organization, originally intended to serve only the local stations, is becoming instead the center of power and the focal point of control for the entire public broadcasting system." As if by rote, Nixon's veto message singled out *Sesame Street* for praise, though even by this early date it was clear that Bert, Ernie, Cookie Monster, and the rest would not vote for Nixon should Muppets ever obtain the franchise. Radio went unmentioned by the President, who cited "localism" as the polestar to which the CPB should return.[42]

Nixon relented when presented with a compromise bill that feinted in the direction of local autonomy. A fight with the CPB was by no means a surefire political winner. As Antonin Scalia explained in a memo, an "attempt to cut back on public broadcasting as a whole would be doomed to failure because of strong support from education interests, minority groups, and liberals, but also from Congressmen whose districts contain stations which contribute to local education."[43] The new breed of educational broadcasters were proving far more politically savvy than their politically hapless forerunners. They had an actual constituency, and they were not afraid to use it. As a result, Scalia foresaw "a long-range problem of significant social consequences—that is, the development of a government-funded broadcast system similar to the BBC"—and implacably anti-conservative.[44]

Republicans, who seemed congenitally suspicious of the Corporation for Public Broadcasting and all its works, departed the White House, and as Democrat Jimmy Carter moved in hopes were high for significantly magnified funding. The Carter-era president of NPR was Democratic operative Frank Mankiewicz, whom one NPR staffer described as "carrying the biggest Rolodex I had ever seen."[45] Mankiewicz was politically savvy but largely ignorant of radio; his was a movie family. (His father wrote the Orson Welles classic film *Citizen Kane*.) But there is ignorance of radio and then there is ignorance of radio: when NPR chairman Edward Elson, an Atlanta gift shop mogul who was in tight with the Jimmy Carter-Bert Lance crowd, had approached Mankiewicz to ask if he'd be interested in applying for the position of president, Mankiewicz reputedly first asked him what NPR was.[46] His intimate political connections, all with the left side of the ideological dial, made him an immediately polarizing figure, and his not always warm and fuzzy personality did not disarm opposition.

Mankiewicz, says Jim Russell, one-time host of *All Things Considered*, had a vision "that was entirely journalistic and not very lyrical."[47] His conception of National Public Radio was all news, heavily DC-oriented, with little if any room for stories of Basque sheepherders in Nevada, tortilla recipes from New Mexico, or tiddlywinks players from Rhode Island. Mankiewicz decried "Snail-Darter Programming," as he termed the catering to ever more exotic mini-segments of the audience.[48] He was an idea man, though, and not averse to innovation; early in his tenure NPR broadcast live gavel-to-gavel coverage of the U.S. Senate debate over the Panama Canal Treaty.

Mankiewicz boasted that NPR's staff had "gone light-years beyond the old 'rip-and-read' school of broadcast journalism." But he insisted that the hard news ought to be delivered without partisan shading. He extolled the "American promise that citizens should have access to a full range of information in an uncensored marketplace of ideas." Far from being a mouthpiece for the liberal wing of the Democratic Party—which Mankiewicz had been, literally, as press secretary for Robert Kennedy's 1968 campaign for the Democratic nomination and director of George McGovern's 1972 presidential campaign—NPR, he said, was determined to report the news "with fairness, impartiality, and without arrogance."[49] Alas, his "hypercompetitive spirit and his lack of financial acumen" proved a nearly fatal combination.[50]

It was during the reign of Mankiewicz that *Morning Edition* was born. *Morning Edition*, as Rick Lewis, deputy director of news, put it in a November 1, 1979, memo introducing the show to NPR affiliates, was more of a "service" than "a new artistic concept." Lewis conceded the similarity to *All Things Considered*, but assured station managers that the differences would be apparent in "personality, pacing, and time of day," with "one previewing and the other reviewing" the events of the day. *Morning Edition* was launched, as Mankiewicz recalled, when CPB president Henry Loomis, a Nixon appointee but an old radio man, offered NPR the entirety of a $15 million windfall at the end of the fiscal year, assuming NPR could find a suitable use for it. Mankiewicz immediately suggested "a morning news program," and when Loomis warned him that this $15 million lagniappe was a one-time thing, and asked the seasoned politico just how he proposed to pay for a second year, Mankiewicz replied, "Blackmail, Henry. I'll go to your board and ask, 'Do you folks want to kill one of the only serious news programs on the air?'" Loomis "laughed," said Mankiewicz, "and told me the check was in the mail."[51]

Frank Mankiewicz was not always quite so keen of vision. In the 1970s, Minnesota Public Radio was producing a quirky, offbeat slice of aural Americana in Garrison Keillor's *Prairie Home Companion*. But Mankiewicz passed on the chance to distribute the show over NPR's satellite system because he perceived it as a "put-down" of rural life. "It would cement our status as elitist," he later said.[52] *Prairie Home Companion*, the variety show straight outta the heart of Minnesota Nice, elitist? Mankiewicz made his case and drew some blood: "I knew it was a yuppie program. I didn't like it. I don't like it now. I think it mocks the values of middle-class America. It's for people who like country and western music, but are ashamed of it. So it mocks the values of the people who create it. I thought it was the *Laverne and Shirley* of public radio programs."[53] Phrased that way, he may have had a point. NPR was also said to deem the show, which later became a pop culture phenomenon, "too narrow and its production values too low for national consumption."[54]

Stemming in part from NPR's refusal to distribute *Prairie Home Companion*, five of the most energetic public radio station producers, led by Minnesota Public

Radio and its president Bill Kling, joined forces in 1982 to distribute their programs via satellite under the banner of American Public Radio Associates, which excised "Associates" the following year and operated as a private entity which "offered programs à la carte, while NPR offered stations its entire program service for a single price." Within two years, the upstart APR, which did not receive direct funding from the CPB but instead relied upon programming fees and support from corporations and foundations, was offering 200 h of programming to stations.[55] St. Paul, Minnesota, had set itself up as a rival to Washington DC. The cheek of those Twin Cities! As if to rub in the fact that APR had an eye on the bottom line, unlike the government-subsidized NPR, one of the first shows it offered (and coproduced) was *Marketplace*, a financial news program.[56]

American Public Radio was redubbed Public Radio International in 1994, partly in recognition of its coproductions with the BBC. Among the other popular programs which NPR refused to distribute and Public Radio International picked up was Ira Glass's *This American Life*. In 2004, Minnesota Public Radio hived off to form American Public Media, whose centerpiece was the marketing gift that seemed to never stop giving, *Prairie Home Companion,* whose swag adorned many an NPR listener's kitchen, that is until Garrison Keillor was #MeToo-ed in 2017 over allegations of sexual improprieties, and he disappeared down the memory hole. He was so thoroughly expunged that it was as if he and the program he conceived and hosted, if not the money they brought in, had never existed.

Public Radio International, as Brian Montopoli noted, "is blessedly free of The Voice"—that arch, faintly supercilious, fake-hesitation elite school cadence that is seemingly *de rigueur* for NPR announcers.[57] Its programs, produced outside the Beltway bubble, just sound different. But so does *Car Talk*, hosted by Ray and Tom Magliozzi, one of the few public radio shows featuring distinctly working-class accents, which has been distributed by NPR since 1987, though 2012 was the last year original episodes were produced. Stoutly atypical, it was for years the most listened-to program on NPR. The Magliozzis of *Car Talk* fame had a garage in that most NPR-ish of cities, Cambridge, Massachusetts.

The Reagan administration came to town with abolition on its mind, or at least in the minds of its more fervent budget-cutters and constitutionalists, but it found in CPB a powerful lobbying force. The Corporation for Public Broadcasting's FY 1982 appropriation of $172 million dipped to $137 million in FY 1983 and then, after a struggle to prevent its further decline, to $130 million in FY 1984. Thus, the CPB survived the onslaught of the early Reagan years, when David Stockman and a small band of true-believing budget-cutters had taken aim at various public subsidies. "This gives us a real chance to stabilize this institution," said CPB president Edward J. Pfister as President Reagan signed a supplemental appropriation bill in July 1982, restoring $24.4 million to the corporation's FY 1984 subsidy.[58] You could almost hear his sigh of relief: the assault had been repelled, and there would be no renewal thereof until a dozen years later.

The Reagan years coincided with a wave of incipient privatization efforts around the globe. Public media were among the targets. As Willard D. Rowland Jr. and Michael Tracey of the University of Colorado noted in their survey of privatization efforts, elements of the global Right questioned the validity of public ownership or subsidy of media, while elements of the global Left had come to regard public broadcasting as a tool of the status quo. The former, they write, would argue that "social good flows not so much from collective activity organized from the top down but from myriad individual decisions organized from the bottom up." Rejecting the assumptions of such national media outfits as the Corporation for Public Broadcasting, the British Broadcasting Corporation, and the Canadian Broadcasting Corporation, which place some measure of responsibility for the education and enlightenment of the citizenry on state actors, the privatizers held that "[n]either the state nor any subsidiary agency, no matter how autonomous, has the right within a democratic society to make choices for its citizens in the electronic, audiovisual area, any more than it has a right to tell them which books or newspapers to read."[59]

Alas, the debate within the Congress has never risen to that level of complexity or perceptiveness. Rather, it annually centers around whose ox is being gored, whose palm is being greased, whose prejudices are being appeased. And so the CPB, BBC, and CBC hum along, having beaten back challenges from as formidable a pair as Ronald Reagan and Margaret Thatcher. The Peacock Committee of 1985–1986, an initiative of British Prime Minister Thatcher, recommended—unsuccessfully—the privatization of BBC Radio 1 and BBC Radio 2, contending that the British should adopt "a system which recognizes that viewers and listeners are the best ultimate judges of their own interests, which they can best satisfy if they have the option of purchasing the broadcasting service they require from as many alternative sources of supply as possible."[60] Three and a half decades later, BBC Radio 1 and BBC Radio 2 remain the Beeb's flagship stations.

Curiously, it was Frank Mankiewicz, the Bobby Kennedy-George McGovern liberal, who envisaged a privately funded future for NPR. Engaging in Reaganite doggerel, Mankiewicz promised to be "off the federal fix by '86."[61] The McGovernite, whose pedigree was probably to the left of any other NPR president, sought to wean it from the federal trough. Mankiewicz's Project Independence, unveiled in late 1981, as the initial danger of Reaganite budget cuts had passed, called for further commercializing NPR by trading on-air mentions for corporate and foundation support. It also envisioned NPR Plus, which would produce classical, jazz, and news programs for which member stations would pay, and NPR Ventures, which would raise funds by selling satellite space. The McGovernite Mankiewicz was seeking to, in effect, privatize public radio, but those blocking his efforts included standard-issue liberals and such paragons of the establishment as Sharon Percy Rockefeller, a powerhouse on the board of the Corporation for Public Broadcasting.

Mankiewicz's vision of a National Public Radio thriving without the financial support of the national government soon dimmed. The 1986 target date of his Project Independence came and went, and Mankiewicz himself was long gone, having resigned in mid-1983 under pressure for what NPR chronicler and effusive admirer Thomas Looker said was "the careless way in which the Mankiewicz administration handled its finances."[62]

The ambitious Project Independence, while admirable in its desire to wean NPR from federal support, was coming up shy of its goal, and combined with the 20%

reduction in the CPB budget due to Reaganite belt-tightening, NPR faced a deficit of at least $6.5 million. (Some estimated it as high as $9 million.) More than a quarter of the staff, or 139 of 442 employees, was laid off.[63] The squeeze was so tight that "NPR came within about forty-eight hours of shutting down in July 1983," when the landlord of its headquarters at 2020 M Street NW in Washington made noises about locking the doors.[64] Rep. John Dingell (D-MI), chairman of the House Energy and Commerce Committee, whose purview included the non-commercial CPB, charged that "NPR officials and the NPR board have been guilty of financial mismanagement." An audit revealed not only the $6.5 million deficit but also rampant neglect or incompetence in the keeping of the books, with "nonexistent or sloppy financial records" and the misuse of $850,000 in taxes withheld from employee paychecks.[65] At least $85,000 in "undocumentable charges" had been run up on NPR American Express cards.[66] Heads were demanded, and a few rolled, most notably that of president Mankiewicz.

Mankiewicz reflected in 2009 that banks were willing to lend money to cover the deficit, but CPB chairwoman Sharon Percy Rockefeller would not guarantee the loans because she was furious that the NPR chieftain had refused to lobby Congress to restore the CPB to full funding. He could not, explained Mankiewicz, "ask for public broadcasting to be made whole when programs like food stamps were being cut."[67] Or this is Mankiewicz's side of the story. He also charged that Percy Rockefeller would not forgive him for "successfully lobbying Congress for a greater percentage of CPB's budget" over her objections. "She never forgot that," Mankiewicz told Mark Huber.[68] The lesson, he said, is that "I should have been nicer to the people at CPB."[69] Wherever the truth resides in the Mankiewicz-Rockefeller squabble, Mankiewicz was out the door, and NPR met its payroll and lived to broadcast another day. Mankiewicz's interim successor, Ron Bornstein, secured a $7 million loan (the line of credit was $8.5 million), and the worst of the crisis was over. A majority of NPR stations (170 of 281) agreed to contribute a portion of their federal grant money in the event NPR could not repay the loan.[70]

Over the objections of many member stations, NPR held a "Drive to Survive" fund-raising campaign over the course of three days in the summer of 1983. News director Barbara Cohen, who balked at the 10% cut proposed by management, was a prime mover in this. Jack Mitchell, then acting as the interim head of NPR's programming department, recalled pointedly, "One hundred influential members of Congress signed a letter to us demanding that we preserve NPR news. Were it not for rules prohibiting reporters from lobbying, I might have suspected that NPR's potent congressional reporting team of [Linda] Wertheimer and [Cokie] Roberts might have had something to do with that letter."[71] Whether they did or not, the letter suggests the close relationship between National Public Radio and the national political figures it covers—sycophantically, if those figures are of the correct political coloration.

Among the reforms borne of the 1983 near-shutdown was a change in the way the CPB funded NPR. Instead of sending public radio's share of its annual appropriation to NPR, henceforth the CPB would cut the checks directly to member stations, which would plenish NPR's coffers by buying the programs it produced. In this way, as former correspondent John Ydstie notes, critics of public radio subsidization such as

1990s House Speaker Newt Gingrich "could not paint the network as a Washington-centric operation. Instead, he had to contend with local member stations from virtually every Congressional district across the country raising their voices to protect funding for their stations."[72] Necessity, mother of invention, was also politically shrewd.

If Frank Mankiewicz came from the moderate left of the Democratic Party, his successor (after the interim Bornstein), Douglas Bennet, whom President Carter had appointed director of the U.S. Agency for International Development, hailed from what Arthur Schlesinger has called the vital center—though it had devitalized somewhat during Bennet's salad days as an aide to Democratic Senators Hubert Humphrey (MN), Thomas Eagleton (MO), and Abraham Ribicoff (CT). He was the consummate Democratic Party insider, "the quintessential bureaucrat," as one staffer put it.[73]

Bennet, who later served as president of Wesleyan University, in which capacity he was both renowned and harshly criticized for his obsession with raising money, was thought to be a competent balancer of the financial books. By the 1980s those books were being significantly affected by the now-ubiquitous fund drives. These beg-athons, which annoy many listeners but may also be seen as a necessary and praiseworthy voluntaristic practice—and a community-building one withal—became a distinguishing feature of NPR, as well as PBS, in this era. As a rule, the ratio of public radio listeners who contribute financially to its operations versus those who don't is somewhere north of 10%.[74]

The often-blatant fundraising, whether through on-air drives or appeals to snobbery, also inspired one of the most entertaining takedowns ever written of public broadcasting, and though author Michael Kinsley, then editor of *Harper's*, concentrated his fire on PBS rather than NPR, it is too good (and germane) a skewering of public broadcasting sanctimony not to quote from liberally. Kinsley, writing in 1983, noted that public TV's Channel 13 in New York City had announced that its programs would include "enhanced underwriting." This would go beyond the then-typical corporate logos (usually of oil companies at what was mockingly known as the Petroleum Broadcasting System; Mobil was half-mockingly called "the thinking man's gasoline"[75]) and stentorian acknowledgements of corporate support to include "high-quality messages" giving a ten-second plug to the underwriter.

"The spectacle of this old hooker announcing that she has discovered a method of going all the way without losing her virginity is pretty comical," wrote Kinsley, "because there's nothing especially 'non-commercial' about public television." (By a fine coincidence, Frank Mankiewicz, in announcing his Project Independence, had cracked that to raise money NPR was going into every profession "except the oldest."[76]) Rather, Kinsley writes, "'Non-commercial' is essentially a commercial marketing strategy. It lends tone, helping to attract viewers and to pry open their checkbooks. It gives corporations a goody-goody bonus for their advertising/underwriting dollar." But it also raises an uncomfortable question for its practitioners: "why should the general taxpayer be subsidizing the entertainment of people who are thought to be likely customers for Piper Heidseick, Gucci, and E. F. Hutton (the three original 'enhanced underwriters' at Channel 13)?"[77]

Kinsley had fun with the ostentatiously elitist marketing strategy: "I recently got a fund-raising letter from Channel 13 appealing to sentiments that are not exactly democratic. 'The responsibility has shifted…to you,' said the letter, referring to recent cuts in government support. To whom? 'To the discriminating minority who really *care* what goes through their eyes and into their minds.' For a contribution of fifty dollars, I was offered 'the THIRTEEN Tote Bag. Carry it proudly. *It's the tote with the most cachet in town.'*"[78] Such appeals are almost beyond parody, until one realizes that *they work.* The percentage of the average station's budget derived from listener donations rose from 8 in 1970 to 20 in 1985[79] and has been as high as 30% in recent years.[80]

Crowding Out or Crowding In?

The appeals to private, individual philanthropy also raise this question, which goes unasked in public debates but is the subject of some contention among academics: Does government spending on social or cultural programs "crowd out" charitable contributions to nonprofits and cultural organizations? Does public subsidy *discourage* private giving?

Arthur S. Brooks, a professor of public administration and economics at Georgia State University and later the president of the center-right think tank the American Enterprise Institute, studied the question in the late 1990s. Advocates of public subsidy have promoted it as "seed money" which primes the soil for munificent private donations. Critics have countered that such subsidies may discourage, or crowd out, private giving, as potential donors figure that the government is already meeting the financial needs of worthy causes and organizations. Brooks found that at lower levels of subsidy, "government support may stimulate private giving, whereas at higher levels it could have just the opposite effect."[81]

An organization or agency which receives a significant portion of its funding from the government will give off a quasi-governmental vibe, and who really wants to donate to a cultural version of the Post Office or the Department of Motor Vehicles? Moreover, substantial governmental assistance can create (or confirm) the impression that the recipient is financially shaky, and thus a dubious investment in the eyes of corporate contributors, who prefer to donate to healthy and sound organizations. Contrariwise, donors may regard an infusion of government seed money as a seal of approval, believing that the imprimatur of Washington is evidence of legitimacy.

Surveying the empirical evidence from various studies, Brooks concluded that "crowding out" is a more common phenomenon than the stimulation of donations, though the crowding-out effect is limited in size.[82] The data from studies in the arts and culture field are "diverse," Brooks says, although the one study devoted to public radio, a 1989 paper by Texas A&M economist Bruce Robert Kingma, discovered a definite crowding-out effect. Kingma's sample comprised 3541 individuals who identified themselves as public radio listeners in 1986 surveys conducted by Audience Research Analysis and the Arbitron Corporation on behalf of the Corporation for Public Broadcasting and National Public Radio. Over half (1783) had contributed to public radio, with an average contribution of $45.[83] The results were clear, even stark: "a $10,000 increase in government funds for public radio results in a $0.15

decrease in an agent's contribution." At the time, the average public radio station had 9000 individual donors or members, so the average crowd-out for a $10,000 increment was $1350.[84]

Following up on Kingma, Arthur Brooks undertook his own investigation into the effect of both subsidies and tax rates upon private contributions to public radio. His data set consisted of all 91 U.S. public radio stations which reported assets in excess of $10 million in 1995, as well as a probability sample of stations below that asset level. Unlike Kingma's finding of a crowding-out effect of government spending, Brooks found that government subsidy of public radio crowded *in* private donations, though these dropped sharply as the level of subsidy increased, and eventually reversed into a crowding-out effect. This was, he admits, "not...typical" in the literature. He concluded that public funding at "low levels may have a leveraging impact on private giving," though a large enough increase in funding has the opposite effect.[85] NPR stations did not respond to this finding by asking Congress to limit their appropriations so as not to discourage private giving.

As Brooks explained, encouragement of charitable contributions via the tax code is a significant source of what he calls "indirect government support" of nonprofits.[86] It is posited by some that hikes in the tax rate are associated with more generous giving, as citizens prefer to direct their monies to causes of their own choosing rather than those of the government's choosing. In fact, an increase in state tax rates, in Brooks's study, *was* correlated with an increase in donation levels to public radio. All else being equal, he writes, "a "one-point increase in the maximum state tax rate corresponds to about 28 cents more in per capita giving."[87] This is not, he hastened to add, an argument for boosting tax rates!

Crowding out can take other forms as well. The old jest that public radio is a "classical music jukebox" has not yet faded to anachronism; listeners in many markets depend on their local NPR station for the classical music that, we are told, simply would not grace the airwaves absent government funding. A 1990s study found that jazz and classical music made up less than 1% (0.6%) of programming by the nation's 9943 commercial stations but that 17.2% of the 1592 noncommercial stations program classical music exclusively, while another 4.5% are devoted solely to jazz.[88] That's why Mr. Conscience of a Conservative, Senator Barry Goldwater (R-AZ), had defended spending federal dollars on radio: "It fills the need for high class programs that the American people can't get through commercial stations."[89]

Or so the assumption goes. Surely highbrow tastes cannot be satisfied absent public subsidy. Right? Yale University economists Steven T. Berry and Joel Waldfogel tested that assumption in a 1997 study which asked of public radio in the United States: "Does It Correct Market Failure or Cannibalize Commercial Stations?" Berry and Waldfogel examined 165 major U.S. markets. In most of the 25 largest, commercial stations as well as public stations programmed classical music, but in only nine of the other 140 were classical airs broadcast over commercial stations.[90] In these larger markets especially, the authors asked, "Do public and commercial classical stations compete for listening share and revenue? Do public stations crowd out commercial stations?"

The authors found "explicit evidence of a crowding out relationship" between public and commercial radio in classical music and, to a lesser extent, jazz.[91] Public, taxpayer-supported stations were competing with private commercial stations in the provision of classical music. The government was, in a sense, subsidizing competitors to private actors and possibly "displac[ing] commercial entry in large markets." More than one-third of "public funding of stations airing jazz and classical music programming is allocated to public stations in the markets which would be served by similar commercial programming in the absence of public broadcasting."[92] So there is significant duplication, or displacement, of classical music formats provided by private broadcast companies, at least in major markets. There is a market, it would seem, for enlightenment, or high culture, that can be met by the private provision of cultural offerings. And, one might argue, the amount of high-culture programming would be undoubtedly larger in the absence of public-broadcast competitors.

There was, indisputably, yet another form of crowding out—literal crowding out—at work during NPR's growth. In 1966, on the eve of the Public Broadcasting Act of 1967, there were 314 educational stations on FM, two-thirds of them under the auspices of colleges and universities, and about half (158) operated at 10 W.[93] These little stations, which ranged from relatively inactive to lively and localist in a very real sense, were left out of the CPB universe. They hadn't the staff, budget, hours, or transmission power to qualify for any kind of subsidy. Others were ineligible because their programming was "designed to further the principles of a particular religious philosophy."[94]

As Scott M. Martin wrote in his monograph on FM educational radio, "As early as 1972, CPB had been convinced that the presence of low-power, nonprofessional stations in the FM band made the attainment of their goals impossible."[95] So it declared war, or at least a simmering hostility, on the 10-watters. By itself, a low-power station presented barely a nuisance to its educational confreres, but in the aggregate, they were said to block the enlargement of stations with grander ambitions.

An earlier generation of populists had championed relatively low-power stations for exactly that reason. Senator Burton K. Wheeler (D-MT), who had been the running mate of Progressive Party candidate Robert LaFollette in 1924, sponsored a successful 1938 U.S. Senate resolution opposing stations of more than 50 kilowatts in power, claiming, as Carl J. Friedrich and Evelyn Sternberg of Harvard University explained in 1943, that "such stations were against the public interests because of their adverse effect on small stations and their tendency to aid concentrations of control." The blare and gab of super-stations, argued the populists, would drown out more authentic expressions of American culture, especially those rooted in rural or small-town areas. The fear, as Friedrich and Sternberg phrased it, was that "programs emanating exclusively from the big cities and talent centers of the country will make New Yorkers and Hollywoodites out of all Americans, and local American music, dancing, and humor will be forgotten."[96] That has, of course, happened, though the reasons for the erasure of local cultures extend well beyond federal radio policies.

The Federal Communications Commission took up the issue in 1978, with an eye to running the pipsqueaks off the dial. Weighing in was the Corporation for Public Broadcasting, which asserted in a petition that low-power Class D stations served no real educational purpose and were, typically, "commercial radio stations without the commercials," broadcasting a steady and non-nutritious diet of popular music.[97] The CPB urged the FCC to demand of these stations a demonstration that they were meeting the educational needs of the community—educational in an NPR sense—or else their licenses would be revoked.

The college students who manned so many of these underdog stations fought back. Their Intercollegiate Broadcasting System (IBS) denied that NPR's was the one true way to enlighten the community, and argued that a volunteer corps of enthusiastic young people were just as valid a staff as paid professionals under the CPB/NPR umbrella. They quoted Henry David Thoreau's *Walden*: "If a man does not keep pace with his companions, perhaps it is because he hears a different drummer. Let him step to the music which he hears, however measured or far away."[98] Those cheeky kids were calling in America's favorite anarchist to do battle with the burgeoning bureaucracy of government radio!

The IBS viewed the whole episode as a grab for empire. "The program diversity which the public now enjoys is to be sacrificed so that CPB produced and sponsored programs can dominate the FM band," they charged.[99] The intent was to squeeze out other voices, other rooms, so that educational radio spoke with a single upper-middle-class suburban liberal accent. That this is what happened testifies to the percipience of the student broadcasters.

The FCC cracked down on the 10-W stations, ordering the removal of Class D stations from the educational FM spectrum. It also set minimum hourly requirements for such stations, though these were suspended during school vacations. The IBS stations responded by upping their power to 100 watts, the Class A range, which proved doable for most stations and, as Scott M. Martin noted, further crowded the spectrum, defeating the purported purpose of the reform.[100]

As the millennium came to a close, NPR teamed up with the National Association of Broadcasters against an FCC rule that would have "issue[d] licenses for low-power FM radio stations to 1000 or more schools, churches, and other small community organizations."[101] (The Davids survived Goliath's onslaught: Beginning in 2000, the FCC and Congress have legalized low-power FM stations (LPFM) which operate below 100 watts as a means of encouraging community radio. NPR has fought, unsuccessfully, against LPFM, though localist advocates of small-scale radio argue that the restrictions remain unnecessarily cumbersome. But the mini-stations exist, to the displeasure of NPR.)

In 1987, Doug Bennet hired Adam Clayton Powell III to head NPR's news division as vice president for news and information, whose bailiwick included *All Things Considered* and *Morning Edition*. Powell, the son of former Harlem Democratic congressman Adam Clayton Powell Jr., was almost immediately unpopular for both his "commercial, mass-market sensibilities" and his "aloof" style.[102] Powell had cut his radio eyeteeth on the commercial side, as a news director and even a station owner, and he precipitated, or experienced, a culture clash. A Congress kid (like Cokie Roberts), he had a DC-centric vision. The news, he believed, was what powerful people did or said in Washington and New York and London and Moscow; stories about butterfly collectors or cowboy poets in Elko, Nevada—the sort of offbeat human-interest stories that some NPR reporters did quite well—Powell regarded as frivolous distractions from the comings and goings and edicts and bombings of the high and mighty.

At antipodes from Powell was someone like Ari Silverman, a then-senior producer for *All Things Considered*, who said, "As much as people need to hear two more reports about Eastern Europe or the Third World, they also need to hear about how to pick rhubarb for a pie. They need to hear a farmer out on his tractor and the sound of a twister coming across the prairie, a dog barking somewhere—things coming at them from the other side of the brain."[103]

The defining moment of Powell's tenure came in 1988, when NPR's foreign editor intended to send three reporters to cover the Reagan-Gorbachev summit in Moscow; Powell, who wanted a contingent of ten, overruled and then fired him. Powell himself was out the door a year or so later. But the gradual shift to the mainstream, and towards what many viewed as stodginess, continued. An NPR correspondent lamented in the late 1980s that the news department was "becoming CBS. The staff walks into their morning meetings with the *New York Times* and the *Washington Post* and it's real easy for that to become their world."[104] As one critic sighed, NPR, whose founders had promised something different, had become "a house organ of respectable inside-the-Beltway liberalism—news written by and for aging yuppies whose idea of adventuresome politics is telling Dan Quayle jokes."[105]

Jay Kernis, who spent over two decades in programming at NPR before decamping for CBS, NBC, and CNN, led a successful de-emphasis on the arts and a focus on news, politics, and other Beltway obsessions. He justified this with the argument that "public radio's future was in making the democracy better and helping citizens become smarter," which is a recipe, of course, for gentle propaganda, as Those Who Know Best shape the stories that are intended to educate We the Benighted.[106] Kernis's post-NPR career is no anomaly; Jack Mitchell remarks, "It's no accident they built the place across from CBS," referring to NPR headquarters. "NPR was made up of people who wanted to work there. It became very Washington-oriented."[107]

Both supporters and critics acknowledged its influence within the corridors of power. There was nothing shaggy or offbeat about the mature NPR. By the 1980s it had become, in the words of journalism professor Michael P. McCauley, author of *NPR: The Trials and Triumphs of National Public Radio*, the "'unofficial bulletin board' for presidents, congressmen, lobbyists, and journalists."[108] The propriety of presidents and congressmen authorizing and appropriating the budget of this bulletin board made critics on both right and left increasingly uneasy, and in many cases harsh.

Old hands were dismayed; the excitement was gone. Humor had become as rare as stories originating from Idaho. A craving for respectability seemed to be the prime motivating force. "Their goal," said former NPR journalist Barbara Newman in 1994, "was to be part of the establishment, and they succeeded."[109] Or in the words of John McChesney, an NPR foreign editor who, after objecting to Powell's summit overkill, left to run an inn in Marin County, California, "I don't see what service you're providing by covering every peristaltic wave in the movement of the bowels of Congress."[110]

This drift into the sludgy and turbid waters of the Washington mainstream was documented by, among others, Alan G. Stavitsky and Timothy W. Gleason of the School of Communication at the University of Oregon. Writing in *Journalism Quarterly*, they related their study of the news programming of both NPR and Pacifica, which had, ostensibly, "alternative" origins. This study of the news coverage of the 90-min *All Things Considered* and the half-hour *Pacifica Radio News* was conducted in late 1991, as NPR had settled squarely into the *New York Times-Washington Post* world and Pacifica was doubling its news budget and ramping up its Washington coverage, prompting one jaundiced observer to liken it to "an aging flower child looking for a mainstream job."[111] By this time, as Westwood One vice president for news (and former Gerald Ford press secretary) Ron Nessen said, "NPR has this image of being the poor relation going up against the big network greats. In fact, NPR's news budget is twice our budget. My feeling is they have an awful lot of money."[112]

They also have a competitive advantage over their unsubsidized private enterprise competitors. Mike Gonzalez quotes Chris Plante, host of Washington DC's commercial radio station WMAL: "Everyone in the radio business knows that when we go to a commercial break, radio listeners around the city are changing the channel. Some come back a few minutes later. Some don't. That reality obviously drives our ratings in a downward direction. NPR never hits that wall. Their ratings in the DC metro are great. Stunning. Liberal area, to be sure. But if CBS didn't have to run commercials, and had commercial-free programming all day and all night because of taxpayer subsidies, that would obviously put ABC and NBC at a terrible competitive disadvantage."[113] And what, really, do ratings—that is, market approval—matter when the popularity or lack thereof of an enterprise has, at least in theory, nothing to do with its financial health? Mara Liasson, an NPR reporter, told *Mother Jones* magazine in the mid-1980s that "One of our problems is that we don't have any competition. We exist in a strange and wonderful vacuum. On the other hand, heads don't roll if the ratings aren't good, but what is to spur us on to greater heights?"[114]

Stavitsky and Gleason found that coverage by the two entities, one private and the other public, though each claiming to some extent a countercultural pedigree, was not identical. Surprisingly, NPR devoted somewhat less coverage (30.3%) to politics and governance than did Pacifica (44.3%), though the latter broadcast more stories concerning war and peace (29.9%) than did the former (20.8%). Arts and media coverage was negligible during Pacifica's half-hour news program (0.09%) as opposed to NPR (9.5%). Pacifica ran considerably more stories with an international focus (32.3%) than did NPR (19.4%). Even more surprising, Pacifica—which had drifted some distance from the vision of its anarchist-pacifist founder Lewis Hill— relied far more on official sources (55.3%) in its news program than did *All Things Considered* (30.9%).[115]

Stavitsky and Gleason ventured that Pacifica's scantier resources may explain its lopsided reliance on Washington types, but they charged that it "is not providing a significant alternative to the mainstream media's heavy reliance upon official sources and government-generated news." They concluded that both news programs were

under the "dominance of the Washington-New York axis," though NPR's geographically disbursed network of affiliates enabled it to run more stories based at some
remove from that axis.[116]

The Pacifica example is telling. Community radio stations were split on the matter
of accepting federal support. Some eagerly leaped at the prospect of badly needed
funds, while others suspected that taking the king's shilling would make them the
king's man: they would forfeit independence and be sucked into a bureaucratic,
rules-heavy world in which the limits of speech, expression, and even format were
circumscribed by people sitting at desks in Washington. By the 1970s, Pacifica had
grown to a five-station network, having added to its Berkeley, Los Angeles, and New
York stations WPFW in Washington and KPFT in Houston. Debates over whether to
accept CPB monies grew contentious; the question was decided in the affirmative. It
was no accident that pacifists, black radicals, right-wing extremists, and subversive
poets began appearing much less often, and a monolithic within-the-pale leftism
came to dominate.

Pacifica's enrollment in the ranks of the federally subsidized stations provoked
cries of protest from elements of the old guard. For instance, veteran radio newsman
and libertarian Lowell Ponte had been "the token right-winger on KPFK, the fig leaf
that station bosses could point to when accused of broadcasting only leftist political
views." Ponte told listeners that he was KPFK's "resident right-wing anarchist."[117]
In the early years, Ponte recalled, the 110,000-W KPFK, whose powerful signal
beams its offerings to listeners from Santa Barbara to the Mexican border, was "genuine free speech radio," welcoming of dissent from any direction, and charmingly
unpredictable, as one was liable to hear literary criticism, science-fiction novelists,
or obscure folk music any time one turned on the station.[118]

Ponte's weekly hour-long show was popular with listeners, according to station-
commissioned polls, but by the late 1970s, says Ponte, the freewheeling vibe of
Pacifica had curdled into what he called "Stalinism." His show was reduced to a
15-min commentary, and then unceremoniously dropped in January 1980, as the
minatory figure of Ronald Reagan rose in the sky and the news director of KPFK
instructed his staff to infuse "class consciousness" into their programming.[119] Ponte
went on to a notable career in Los Angeles-area radio, and he spoke fondly of the
friends and memories he had made in KPFK's freewheeling days, but in the early
1990s, as the Corporation for Public Broadcasting came under the fiercest attack
it would ever—at least as of this writing—weather, he objected to the then-annual
$134,000 subsidy the station was receiving from the CPB.[120]

His remarks echoed those of Thomas Jefferson in the Virginia Statute for Religious
Freedom: "to compel a man to furnish contributions of money for the propagation
of opinions which he disbelieves and abhors, is sinful and tyrannical."[121] Now it is
true that Jefferson is a dead white man and thus suspect, but the sentiments have a
timeless quality to them.

Why, Lowell Ponte asked, "should you or I be taxed to broadcast the eccentric—
but in most instances far leftist—views of the elite selected to voice their opinions on
Pacifica Radio[?] … Let KPFK and the other Pacifica stations remain on the air so
long as listeners support them voluntarily. But in the name of free-speech radio, we

should eliminate the tax subsidy you and I have been forced to pay to keep KPFK's left-polarized signal on the air."[122]

Pacifica founder Lewis Hill may have agreed, but the hierarchs running the station he had envisaged as a free-speech haven of the radio did not. An era had been shuttered.

Notes of Chapter

1. Barnouw, *Tube of Plenty: The Evolution of American Television*, pp. 398–399.
2. Gibson, *Public Broadcasting: The Role of the Federal Government, 1912–1976*, p. 146.
3. James Day, *The Vanishing Vision: The Inside Story of Public Television* (Berkeley, CA: University of California Press, 1995), endnotes.
4. Gibson, *Public Broadcasting: The Role of the Federal Government, 1912–1976*, p. 149.
5. Ibid., p. 150.
6. Anna Kosof, "Public Radio—Americans Want More," in *Radio: The Forgotten Medium*, edited by Edward C. Pease and Everette E. Dennis (New Brunswick, NJ: Transaction, 1997/1995), p. 173.
7. Mitchell, *Listener Supported: The Culture and History of Public Radio*, p. 45.
8. Michael P. McCauley, *NPR: The Trials and Triumphs of National Public Radio* (New York: Columbia University Press, 2005), p. 22.
9. Mitchell, *Listener Supported: The Culture and History of Public Radio*, p. 45.
10. See "The Public Radio Study, 1969," *Current*, https://current.org/1969/04/the-public-radio-study-1969/, accessed July 9, 2019.
11. Richard Kostelanetz, "The New Benefactors," *Liberty* (January 1990): 60.
12. "Public Broadcasting Act of 1967," 47 U.S.C. 96.
13. Gibson, *Public Broadcasting: The Role of the Federal Government, 1912–1976*, p. 158.
14. Ibid., p. 172.
15. "Public Broadcasting: Controversy Over Federal Role," *Congressional Quarterly* (December 11, 1971): 2567.
16. Engelman, *Public Radio and Television in America: A Political History*, p. 92.
17. Mitchell, *Listener Supported: The Culture and History of Public Radio*, p. ix.
18. Noah Adams, "And Radio," *This is NPR: The First Forty Years*, p. 23.
19. Herman W. Land Associates, *The Hidden Medium: A Status Report on Educational Radio in the United States*, p. SP-17.
20. Mitchell, *Listener Supported: The Culture and History of Public Radio*, p. 50.
21. "Bill Siemering's 'National Public Radio Purposes,' 1970," www.current.org, May 17, 2012.
22. *This is NPR: The First Forty Years*, p. 4.
23. "Bill Siemering's 'National Public Radio Purposes,' 1970," www.current.org.
24. Adam Bernstein, "Donald R. Quayle, first president of National Public Radio, dies at 84," *Washington Post*, April 21, 2015.
25. Mitchell, *Listener Supported: The Culture and History of Public Radio*, p. 65.

26.   Joseph P. Duggan, "Some Things Considered," *The Alternative: An American Spectator* (March 1977): 13.
27.   Cokie Roberts, "Foreword: Radio Has the Best Pictures," in *This is NPR: The First Forty Years*, p. 9.
28.   Nicols Fox, "Public Radio's Air Wars," *Columbia Journalism Review* (January/February 1992).
29.   *This is NPR: The First Forty Years*, p. 25.
30.   Duggan, "Some Things Considered," *The Alternative: An American Spectator*: 15.
31.   Gibson, *Public Broadcasting: The Role of the Federal Government, 1912– 1976*, pp. 171, 189.
32.   Chase, "Public Broadcasting and the Problem of Government Influence: Towards a Legislative Solution," *University of Michigan Journal of Law Reform*: 86.
33.   "Public Broadcasting: Controversy Over Federal Role," *Congressional Quarterly* (December 11, 1971): 2567.
34.   Ibid.: 2569.
35.   Day, *The Vanishing Vision: The Inside Story of Public Television*, p. 218.
36.   Steven D. Zansberg, "'Objectivity and Balance' in Public Broadcasting: Unwise, Unworkable, and Unconstitutional," *Yale Law & Policy Review*, Vol. 12 (1994): 195.
37.   Chase, "Public Broadcasting and the Problem of Government Influence: Towards a Legislative Solution," *University of Michigan Journal of Law Reform*: 86.
38.   Patrick J. Buchanan, *Nixon's White House Wars: The Battles That Made and Broke a President and Divided America Forever* (New York: Crown Forum, 2017), p. 273.
39.   Mitchell, *Listener Supported: The Culture and History of Public Radio*, p. 163.
40.   Gibson, *Public Broadcasting: The Role of the Federal Government, 1912– 1976*, p. 154.
41.   The CPB received one-year authorizations until 1973, when it doubled to two years, and two years later these were extended to three years.
42.   "Message from the President of the United States, Vetoing H.R. 13918— House Document 92-320," U.S. House of Representatives, 92nd, Congress, 2nd session, June 30, 1972.
43.   Charles S. Clark, "Public Broadcasting," *CQ Researcher* (September 18, 1992): 7.
44.   Gonzalez, "Is There Any Justification for Continuing to Ask Taxpayers to Fund NPR and PBS?" Knight Foundation.
45.   Adams, "And Radio," *This is NPR: The First Forty Years*, p. 48.
46.   David A. Vise, "Edward E. Elson: An Empire Built On a Simple Idea," *Washington Post*, February 2, 1986; Robert K. Avery and Robert Pepper, "Balancing the Equation: Public Radio Comes of Age," *Public Telecommunications Review* (March/April 1979): 28.

47. *This is NPR: The First Forty Years*, p. 68.
48. Mark Huber, "The Static at National Public Radio," Heritage Foundation, June 17, 1985.
49. Larry Josephson, editor, *Telling the Story: The National Public Radio Guide to Radio Journalism* (Dubuque, IA: Kendall/Hunt Publishing Co., 1983), p. vii.
50. McCauley, *NPR: The Trials and Triumphs of National Public Radio*, p. 8.
51. *This is NPR: The First Forty Years*, pp. 59–60. In November 1985, NPR launched *Weekend Edition*, a Saturday morning show which later bifurcated into *Weekend Edition Saturday* and *Weekend Edition Sunday*.
52. Ibid., p. 102.
53. McCauley, *NPR: The Trials and Triumphs of National Public Radio*, p. 53.
54. Stephen L. Salyer, "Monopoly to Marketplace—Competition Comes to Public Radio," in *Radio: The Forgotten Medium*, p. 186.
55. Ibid., pp. 187–188.
56. Fox, "Public Radio's Air Wars," *Columbia Journalism Review*: 9–10.
57. Brian Montopoli, "All Things Considerate," *Washington Monthly*, January 1, 2003, www.washingtonmonthly.com.
58. "Public Broadcasting Wins Struggle for '84 Funds," *New York Times*, July 20, 1982.
59. Willard D. Rowland Jr. and Michael Tracey, "Worldwide Challenges to Public Service Broadcasting," *Journal of Communication*, Vol. 40, No. 2 (Spring 1990): 13.
60. Ibid.: 14.
61. Mitchell, *Listener Supported: The Culture and History of Public Radio*, p. 103.
62. Thomas Looker, *The Sound and the Story: NPR and the Art of Radio* (Boston: Houghton Mifflin, 1995), p. 132.
63. Lawrence Zuckerman, "Has Success Spoiled NPR?" *Mother Jones* (June/July 1987): 37.
64. *This is NPR: The First Forty Years*, p. 112. In later, flusher times, the headquarters were moved to 635 Massachusetts Avenue NW and then, in 2013, to 1111 North Capitol Street.
65. Jacqueline Trescott, "NPR 'Financial Mismanagement' Decried," *Washington Post*, June 18, 1983.
66. Huber, "The Static at National Public Radio," Heritage Foundation.
67. *This is NPR: The First Forty Years*, p. 114.
68. Huber, "The Static at National Public Radio," Heritage Foundation.
69. Nicols Fox, "NPR Grows Up," *American Journalism Review* (September 1991).
70. Sally Bedell Smith, "Loan is Approved for Public Radio," *New York Times*, July 29, 1983.
71. Mitchell, *Listener Supported: The Culture and History of Public Radio*, p. 109.
72. *This is NPR: The First Forty Years*, p. 117.

73.   Zuckerman, "Has Success Spoiled NPR?" *Mother Jones*: 36.
74.   The ratio of contributors to noncontributors was 1.6–10.9 million in 1993; 2.2–18.2 million in 2001; and 2.4–22.5 million in 2009. *This is NPR: The First Forty Years*, p. 227. About 10% of listeners offer financial support to public-radio stations. Kosof, "Public Radio—Americans Want More," in *Radio: The Forgotten Medium*, p. 175.
75.   Clark, "Public Broadcasting," *CQ Researcher*: 8.
76.   Zuckerman, "Has Success Spoiled NPR?" *Mother Jones*: 36.
77.   Michael Kinsley, "None Dare Call it Commercial," *Harper's* (March 1, 1983): 9.
78.   Ibid.: 12.
79.   Mitchell, *Listener Supported: The Culture and History of Public Radio*, p. 121.
80.   Lauren Kirchner, "Don't Forget the Facts About NPR Fundraising," *Columbia Journalism Review* (October 28, 2010).
81.   Arthur C. Brooks, "Public Subsidies and Charitable Giving: Crowding out, Crowding in, or Both?" *Journal of Policy Analysis and Management*, Vol. 19, No. 3 (2000): 451–452. See also Jerald Schiff, "Does Government Spending Crowd Out Charitable Contributions?" *National Tax Journal*, Vol. 38, No. 4 (December 1985): 535–546.
82.   Arthur C. Brooks, "Is There a Dark Side to Government Support for Nonprofits?" *Public Administration Review*, Vol. 60, No. 3 (May/June 2000): 211.
83.   Bruce Robert Kingma, "An Accurate Measurement of the Crowd-out Effect, Income Effect, and Price Effect for Charitable Contributions," *Journal of Political Economy*, Vol. 97, No. 5 (October 1989): 1201.
84.   Ibid.: 1203.
85.   Arthur C. Brooks, "Taxes, Subsidies, and Listeners Like You: Public Policy and Contributions to Public Radio," *Public Administration Review*, Vol. 63, No. 5 (September/October 2003): 558–559.
86.   Ibid.: 554.
87.   Ibid.: 558.
88.   Kosof, "Public Radio—Americans Want More," in *Radio: The Forgotten Medium*, p. 174.
89.   Huber, "The Static at National Public Radio," Heritage Foundation.
90.   Steven T. Berry and Joel Waldfogel, "Public Radio in the United States: Does it Correct Market Failure or Cannibalize Commercial Stations?" National Bureau of Economic Research, Working Paper 6057, Cambridge, MA, June 1997, p. 1.
91.   Ibid., p. 2.
92.   Ibid., pp. 22, 26.
93.   Burke, *An Historical-Analytical Study of the Legislative and Political Origins of the Public Broadcasting Act of 1967*, p. 20. Scott M. Martin, "Educational FM Radio—The Failure of Reform," *Federal Communications Law Journal*, Vol. 34, No. 3 (1982): 436.

94. Duggan, "Some Things Considered," *The Alternative: An American Spectator*: 14.
95. Martin, "Educational FM Radio—The Failure of Reform," *Federal Communications Law Journal*: 436.
96. Friedrich and Sternberg, "Congress and the Control of Radio Broadcasting, I," *American Political Science Review*: 813.
97. Martin, "Educational FM Radio—The Failure of Reform," *Federal Communications Law Journal*: 440.
98. Ibid.: 443.
99. Ibid.: 445.
100. Ibid.: 452.
101. David Barsamian, *The Decline and Fall of Public Broadcasting* (Cambridge, MA: South End Press, 2001), p. 55.
102. *This is NPR: The First Forty Years*, p. 138. Carol Matlack, "Adding a Harder Edge to Public Radio's News," *National Journal* (December 2, 1989): 2951.
103. Bruce Porter, "Has Success Spoiled NPR?" *Columbia Journalism Review* (September/October 1990): 26–27.
104. Alan G. Stavitsky and Timothy W. Gleason, "Alternative Things Considered: A Comparison of National Public Radio and Pacifica Radio News Coverage," *Journalism Quarterly*, Vol. 71, No. 4 (Winter 1994): 777–778.
105. Glenn Garvin, "How Do I Loathe NPR? Let Me Count the Ways," *Liberty*, Vol. 6, No. 6 (August 1993): 44.
106. *This is NPR: The First Forty Years*, p. 230.
107. Zuckerman, "Has Success Spoiled NPR?" *Mother Jones*: 35.
108. McCauley, *NPR: The Trials and Triumphs of National Public Radio*, p. 85.
109. Sam Husseini, "The Broken Promise of Public Radio," *The Humanist* (September/October 1994): 27.
110. Porter, "Has Success Spoiled NPR?" *Columbia Journalism Review*: 29.
111. Stavitsky and Gleason, "Alternative Things Considered: A Comparison of National Public Radio and Pacifica Radio News Coverage," *Journalism Quarterly*: 777.
112. Fox, "NPR Grows Up," *American Journalism Review*.
113. Gonzalez, "Is There Any Justification for Continuing to Ask Taxpayers to Fund NPR and PBS?" Knight Foundation.
114. Zuckerman, "Has Success Spoiled NPR?" *Mother Jones*: 34.
115. Stavitsky and Gleason, "Alternative Things Considered: A Comparison of National Public Radio and Pacifica Radio News Coverage," *Journalism Quarterly*: 778–779.
116. Ibid.: 780.
117. Lowell Ponte, "My Life and Times at Pacifica Radio," in *Public Broadcasting and the Public Trust*, edited by David Horowitz and Laurence Jarvik (Los Angeles: Center for the Study of Popular Culture, 1995), p. 217.
118. Ibid., p. 216.
119. Ibid., p. 218.
120. Ibid., p. 220.

121. "Virginia Statute for Religious Freedom," https://www.monticello.org/site/
      research-and-collections/virginia-statute-religious-freedom.
122. Ponte, "My Life and Times at Pacifica Radio," in *Public Broadcasting and
      the Public Trust*, p. 221.

Chapter 6
Left, Right, or Always Establishment? The Bias Issue

The concern expressed by conservative critics of the Public Broadcasting Act of 1967 that its media progeny would exhibit "definite ideological biases" has been vindicated. It's not that NPR's editors, executives, and reporters meet at 6 a.m. each weekday to plot the day's skewed coverage of events. It is, rather, as Glenn Garvin writes, "that the newsroom is composed almost entirely of like-minded people who share one another's major philosophical precepts."[1] They do not acknowledge their bias because they do not apprehend their bias; their worldview, shared by all with whom they come into professional contact, admits of no other legitimate vantage points. Alternatives thereto exist, seemingly, only in the fever swamps of the alt-Right or the violence-prone communes of the Antifa Left.

Christopher Kirk, executive producer of *All Things Considered* from 1979 to 1981, emphasized the importance of "objectivity and fairness," instructing his staff to "[b]end over backwards to hear all sides and make a particular point of trying to understand the arguments of those with whom you disagree. Try to take everyone's point of view into account."[2] Worthy goals, though one may listen to stories today on *All Things Considered* about, say, immigration or the transgender movement, and search in vain for even the tiniest shred of evidence that critics thereof are motivated by anything other than vile bigotry.

The "NPR Journalist's Code of Ethics and Practices" enjoins "fair, unbiased, accurate, complete and honest" reportage. These first two are of special interest here. "Fair," according to the code, "means that we present all important views on a subject," and "at all times the commitment to presenting all important views must be conscious and affirmative." "Unbiased," the code continues, "means that we separate our personal opinions—such as an individual's religious belief or political ideology—from the subjects we are covering. We do not approach any coverage with overt or hidden agendas."[3] A rigorous lack of bias was not evident in NPR's treatment of the presidency of Ronald Reagan, particularly in his first two years, when "Ronnie Ray-Gun" haunted the dreams of Washington liberals. The Reaganite Heritage Foundation, no exemplar of unbiasedness itself—though as a privately funded organization it had no such obligation—reported on the almost comically

J. T. Bennett, *The History and Politics of Public Radio*, Studies in Public Choice 41, https://doi.org/10.1007/978-3-030-80019-2_6

unbalanced coverage afforded the first-term Reagan. For instance, on July 28, 1981, as the Reagan tax cut was about to be approved by the U.S. House of Representatives, NPR's report began with these quotes:

> Man #1: Let's put it this way. He's strictly big business. That's all he's worried about.
>
> Woman: He's strictly for the rich. He's not for the poor.
>
> Man #2: He's more for the millionaire, the moneyman. You can see it from the friends that he has and the people that he spends his time with.
>
> NPR reporter: The name, not quite taken in vain, is President Reagan. The people live in Pennsylvania. They used to be Reagan supporters. The issue is the Republican tax cut plan.

As Heritage's Benjamin Hart writes, "In this segment, NPR quoted no one who supported the President's plan."[4] The alleged dissatisfaction of Reagan voters with the Reagan economic plan did not keep President Reagan from winning the Keystone State's 25 electoral votes by a margin of 53–46% during his 1984 reelection.

The right-wing media watchdog Accuracy in Media (AIM) predictably took aim at NPR for its "unrelenting left-wing slant with a distinctly nutty twist." (That *nutty twist* sounds like an advertisement for a candy bar.) AIM undertook the favorite project of all media watchdogs, left and right: the monitoring of programs (in this case *All Things Considered* and *Morning Edition*) over a limited period of time (in this case selected days between 1983 and 1985). Reflecting its hawkish Cold War orientation, AIM was particularly exercised over NPR's perceived dovishness. It charged the programs in question with blinkered coverage of unrest in Central America, specifically El Salvador and Nicaragua (or "Nee-Kah-Rah-Wa," in NPR-speak); apartheid in South Africa; and the Soviet invasion and occupation of Afghanistan.[5]

When conservatives complained about NPR's harsh treatment of Reagan, news director Robert Siegel replied, "If Reagan's statements are factually incorrect, it's our obligation to point that out." True, true. But then he added, "If there's a bias against conservatives in the news media in general, I blame a certain strain of conservative for that, one that is anti-intellectual."[6] Yet fact-checking when it comes to the assertions of, say, Bernie Sanders has been conspicuously absent.[7]

Siegel's trope comes straight from the Richard Hofstadter School of psychohistory-ography, in which conservatives, right-wing populists, libertarians, and pretty much anyone who dissents from Vital Center liberalism is either paranoid, status-anxious, or an ignoramus who is easy prey for demagogues. On the other hand, Siegel also admitted that when he became news director in 1983, he sensed a disconnect between NPR and the American citizenry: "Are we describing the country that elected Ronald Reagan? In some ways we weren't. I felt we were perhaps reporting more of a sentimentalized version of the news."[8] (*Sentimentalized* is an odd synonym for liberal, but point taken.)

Defenders of NPR belittled critics as "right-wing ideologues," thus dismissing sound and solid objections to the network's indisputable bias.[9] For one might listen in vain for many years to Terry Gross's *Fresh Air* or *All Things Considered* waiting for a sympathetic portrait or account of, say, a religious person who objects to same-sex marriage or legal abortion or, more recently, transgenderism. This imbalance—this absence or minimization of voices that dissent from the establishment liberalism of the *New York Times* and the *Washington Post*—was not part of the blueprint of the founders. As Bill Siemering said in retrospect, "We were radicals for radio and more inclusive journalism, not for any political agenda."[10]

The wave of criticism from the Right during the Reagan years threw NPR on the defensive, at least for a while. Perhaps the most discussed such criticism was leveled by Fred Barnes in 1986 in the pages of *The New Republic*. There was little new in Barnes's critique, which focused heavily on his magazine's then-current obsession with U.S. policy in Central America. National Public Radio, Barnes charged, was "palpably slanted" in its news coverage. It was sympathetic to the Marxist Sandinistas of Nicaragua and dismissive of the opposition, both the *Somocista* restorationists and the more democratic rebels. He cited specific reports and correspondents in what was a fairly convincing, if not exactly new, indictment. He also repeated the frequent and justified complaint that NPR identified some people on the Right as "ultraconservatives" but tended to call liberals "activists."[11]

Giving heft to Barnes's argument was its venue: *The New Republic*, venerable flagship of twentieth-century American liberalism, though its hawkish tilt under then-owner Martin Peretz had perhaps escaped the notice of NPR's administrators. Charges of blatant bias from a respected weekly of the neoliberal establishment were taken more seriously than howls of outrage from the usual suspects on the "ultraconservative" Right. In response to Fred Barnes's article, NPR vice president Siegel distributed a memo to his news staff stating, "We are not in politics…. We gather information. We verify it. We solicit interesting commentary on it. We have no 'policy' on Central America, or Tax Reform, or South Africa sanctions. We….leave a lot of ourselves at the doorstep when we enter: Religious beliefs; political convictions; financial interests."[12] But just saying does not make it so.

The anti-conservative Republican bias of NPR was so apparent, so surface-level, that one wonders why anyone ever bothered gainsaying it. David Boaz of the Cato Institute proposed this little thought experiment: "[T]ake the long and glowing reviews [on NPR] of two leftist agitprop plays, one written by [former Clinton Secretary of Labor] Robert Reich and performed on Cape Cod and another written by David Hare and performed in Los Angeles. I think we can be confident that if a Reagan Cabinet official wrote a play about how stupid and evil liberals are—the mirror image of Reich's play—it would not be celebrated on NPR."[13]

The libertarian Boaz aside, Reagan-era conservatives seemed more exercised by the political tilt of public broadcasting than they did by its very existence. A year after the Benjamin Hart article for the Heritage Foundation's house organ, *Policy Review*, the foundation published Mark Huber's study "The Static at National Public Radio," in which he led with the complaint that some segments of popular programs were "openly hostile toward the Reagan Administration" and had featured such leftists as the Beat poet Allen Ginsberg; Fred Wertheimer, president of the liberal reform group Common Cause; and Democratic Socialists of America founding member Michael Harrington. The only right-of-center NPR commentators he identified were John McLaughlin and Donald Lambro.[14] The imbalance was significant, and there was the nettlesome fact that NPR regularly quoted Wertheimer, whose wife Linda was an NPR reporter. (Douglas Bennet denied that this was a violation of journalistic ethics.)

Yet had the imbalance been reversed, one sometimes got the sense in the 1980s that Reaganites would not have minded one bit, and would have ardently supported a CPB funding boost. It all depended on whose ox was being gored.

Scholarly support for the conservative lament about NPR bias was supplied in a 1989 study by Professor Mary S. Larson of Northern Illinois University. Relating her findings in *Presidential Studies Quarterly*, Professor Larson explained that she had randomly selected 25 *All Things Considered* broadcasts from every other fiscal year from 1974 to 1983. She examined *ATC*'s coverage of Presidents Ford, Carter, and Reagan, coding them as favorable, neutral, and unfavorable. The results were striking. The coverage of President Ford by *All Things Considered* was "overwhelmingly negative," with three times as many unfavorable as favorable stories. The favorable-unfavorable balance was nearly even with respect to coverage of President Carter by *ATC*, while "twice as much time was devoted to stories unfavorable" to President Reagan as were devoted to stories favorable to Reagan.[15] Larson's conclusion? "NPR has fairly consistently covered the Democratic president less negatively than the Republican presidents."[16]

Curiously, *ATC*'s treatment of Ford was harsher than its treatment of Reagan, despite Ford's relative moderation and Reagan's—to use an NPR term—*ultraconservatism*. We might speculate that this is due to heightened sensitivity to the complaints by the Republican Right, and the awareness on the part of NPR that the Reaganites represented a genuine threat to CPB funding, unlike the Ford Republicans, whose bark and bite were tepid. By the time George H. W. Bush moved into the White House, beating back defunding efforts had become old hat at the CPB. Critics had been reduced to fighting a rearguard action. In 1992, Senator Bob Dole advocated a simple freeze of funds, characterizing the CPB as a nest of "big private profits from a so-called nonprofit network; big bureaucracies and big salaries...and the steady stream of documentary cheerleading for left-wing interests."[17] "[L]iberals love it," he charged. "That's why they are voting for more money. They have their own network."[18] He added, "Every time I turn on NPR, I think I'm listening to the Democratic National Committee."[19]

But this seemed half-hearted; no one really believed that the moderate Dole, a fixture of the Washington establishment, gave two hoots about PBS or NPR, except as their coverage might be critical of his own aspirations to the presidency. As was the case with GOP assaults on the CPB under Presidents Nixon and Reagan, this late-G. H. W. Bush push concentrated on PBS and largely ignored NPR. By now, even Senator Jesse Helms, bête-noire to late twentieth century liberals, conceded that "For the most part, I would acknowledge PBS provides valuable service," but he contended that it was "not balanced."[20] Surely this was a disappointing performance for liberal direct-mail mavens, who in the past had counted on right-wing red meat from Senator Helms to galvanize their fund-raising efforts.

Dole's freeze failed: Congress reauthorized the CPB at levels of $310 million in FY 1994, $375 million in FY 1995, and $425 million in FY 1996. But critics did succeed in attaching an amendment to the reauthorization bill requiring CPB to assess its programming on a regular basis for "quality, diversity, creativity, excellence, innovation, objectivity and balance."[21] It was those last two standards—which had been enshrined in the 1967 legislation creating the CPB but had lacked any means of enforcement—that nettled. For the first time, Congress had directed the CPB to take the necessary steps to meet its "responsibility" in ensuring "objectivity and balance in programming of a controversial nature."[22]

Opponents of the requirement argued that it was unworkable and costly and threatened "infringement of the freedom of speech." Others suggested that balance and objectivity were not even desirable goals, as public broadcasting's purpose was to offer alternatives to the ideas most often vended in the commercial marketplace. The U.S. House of Representatives' report on the Public Broadcasting Act of 1967 stated that CPB support would "enable the non-commercial educational broadcast stations to provide supplementary analysis of the meaning of events already covered by commercial newscasters."[23] The implication—not necessarily inaccurate—was that the three networks largely framed issues through the same lens; the other implication—not necessarily accurate—was that CPB-sponsored newscasts would not.[24]

But Bob Dole wasn't done milking NPR's leftward bias for his own political advantage. He harshly criticized NPR in 1994 for commissioning commentaries from convicted cop-killer and writer Mumia Abu-Jamal. "The last time I checked," said Senator Dole, "we were trying to fight crime, not promote the fortunes of convicted murderers through taxpayer-supported public broadcasting."[25] NPR backed down; Abu-Jamal's series of ten commentaries was dropped. But Dole warned officials that such errors of judgment in the future could subject public radio to enhanced oversight from those who pay the bills.

For good measure, the 1992 Republican Party platform on which George H. W. Bush had waged his unsuccessful campaign for reelection against Governor Bill Clinton of Arkansas declared, "We deplore the blatant political bias of the government sponsored radio and television networks. It is especially outrageous that taxpayers are now forced to underwrite this biased broadcasting through the Corporation for Public Broadcasting....We look forward to the day when public broadcasting is self-sufficient."[26] Stern, but falling well short of a call for abolition.

Ironically, George H. W. Bush's Gulf War of 1991 had been a bonanza for National Public Radio. According to an NPR-produced history of itself, the Gulf War was a veritable windfall, bringing in "a million new listeners to NPR News, at the time when its reach was just 7 million." In fact, for the first time, local affiliates tacked on a surcharge to their own fund-raising in order to finance NPR's war coverage. In exchange for their tax-deductible gift, donors received a t-shirt depicting "planes dropping microphones, beneath the words *Air Superiority*."[27] It was a long way from the sympathetic coverage NPR had given to anti-Vietnam War demonstrations just two decades earlier. In public radio's age of maturity, wars were an opportunity to expand listenership more than to heighten the dudgeon of their already anti-war audience members. This increased emphasis on hard news, on covering the same national and international stories that everyone else covered, pulled NPR ever further from its early and shaggy days, when the discursive and the offbeat made occasional welcome appearances, and it raised the question of why the government should be endowing a media source to cover the government and the government's wars.

(A decade later, in 2001, NPR accepted $170,000 in advertising—oops: make that underwriting—from the government of Kuwait. The announcement went: "The State of Kuwait, in memory of the tenth anniversary of Kuwait's liberation. On the web at Kuwait Thanks America.org."[28] As David Barsamian notes, the outcry over Kuwaiti sponsorship forced NPR to cease accepting sponsorships from Kuwait and other foreign governments. It did, however, continue to run advertisements in all but name by sponsoring corporations, or rather *underwriters*.)

In July 1991, an NPR producer who asked to remain anonymous out of concern for his job wrote PBS fixture Bill Moyers in response to a piece Moyers had written on the subject of PBS's bias, or lack thereof, for *Current*, a publication dedicated to reporting on public broadcasting. "I'd have preferred to respond to you in the pages of *Current*," wrote Moyers's correspondent, "but I'd lose my job if I did so, since my own politically incorrect beliefs ride at the back of the public broadcasting bus." This was no paranoia, he insisted; when, several years earlier, the editor of *Current* had solicited from this writer an editorial on the political slant of public broadcasting, the conservative was told by management at his station that he should "beware my [*sic*] job" should he go public with his complaints.[29]

In his letter to Moyers, the producer bewailed the "monolithic ideological conformity" of public broadcasting. He explained: "When there's nobody in the newsroom to challenge the conventional wisdom—or when those who can are afraid to speak up—opinions pass for facts, catchwords and slogans pass for reasoning. When a newsroom reaches a certain critical mass of people with identical world views, they find it inordinately difficult even to imagine seeing existence from a different angle. They can't even perceive their own uniformity. One of the ironies of my job is to work daily with people who cherish a self-image as iconoclasts, nonconformists, and heretics when in fact they are drearily orthodox on any question you care to name. The very fact that a conservative public-radio producer is regarded by his colleagues as a kind of walking oxymoron is a dead giveaway."[30]

Moyers's reply was gracious if not particularly helpful. He professed unfamiliarity with the broader world of public radio but did say that "I wish there were more like you in our 'universe,' and more like me, too, and of others as well. I don't know if the result would be more liberal or conservative, but I do know it would be more—well, public."[31]

The anti-NPR sentiment among conservatives and libertarians reached its acme in the early to mid-1990s. In their view, Washington-based NPR legal affairs correspondent Nina Totenberg had acted as the transmission belt for scandalous stories about Republican Supreme Court nominees Douglas Ginsburg and Clarence Thomas. Totenberg, though a child of some privilege—her father was a concert violinist—had come up in journalism the old-fashioned way. She dropped out of Boston University before her senior year and worked for such newspapers as the *Boston Record American* and the *Peabody Times* before moving to her mecca, Washington DC, and writing for *Roll Call* and the *National Observer*. She was fired from the latter in 1972 for plagiarism, specifically for borrowing quotes without attribution from the *Washington Post*.[32]

In the 1987 Douglas Ginsburg case, Totenberg had broken what now seems like a dog-bites-man story: the nominee, then a U.S. Court of Appeals judge, had smoked marijuana when he was a law professor at Harvard. Even among journalists and news organizations typically unsympathetic to libertarian-inclined conservatives like Ginsburg, the revelation of the nominee's pot smoking, the resultant media hysteria, and Ginsburg's subsequent withdrawal from consideration were flaming examples of "journalistic moralism run amok" and "neo-Puritanism," as the *Los Angeles Times* reported.[33]

John Hockenberry, long-time NPR general assignment reporter and later an ABC news correspondent, has written amusingly of Totenberg's healthy ego. He praised her nose for news—"Nina got stories no one else in the business did"—but he recalled, with a kind of grinning asperity, the way that she choreographed interviews with the hosts of *All Things Considered*. Hockenberry was guest-hosting *ATC* when Totenberg broke the Ginsburg story, or non-story. (As Hockenberry admitted, "the idea of smoking marijuana disqualifying someone for a job cut a little close to home over at NPR."[34]) The *ATC* producer told Hockenberry just before air time that the show would lead with a chat with Totenberg. "The interview was completely written out," recalled Hockenberry. "Nina always insisted on writing the questions and the answers in such a way that the interviewer appeared to know absolutely nothing while Nina knew everything." In this instance, the first couple of questions were vague and softball-ish. "Just leave them as they are," Totenberg "yelled" when Hockenberry asked for clarification before going on air. The third question she had written was "Did you find anything else, Nina?" which Hockenberry thought "the stupidest question in the history of radio." He considered making it somewhat more specific but "Nina eyed me with her signature glare, warning me off any deviation from the script."[35] Hockenberry played his part, Totenberg spilled the beans, and there would be no Justice Ginsburg.

In 1991, Totenberg revealed that University of Oklahoma law professor Anita Hill had told the FBI, in a confidential interview, of alleged sexual harassment by U.S. Supreme Court nominee Clarence Thomas when Thomas was her superior at the U.S. Department of Education and the Equal Employment Opportunity Commission. The story was actually broken by *Newsday*'s Timothy Phelps, but in a "peculiar twist," as Gay Jervey wrote in *The American Lawyer*, "the glory has gone to Totenberg," who was not inclined to share the credit.[36]

After avidly pursuing the story of Clarence Thomas's alleged sexual harassment and Douglas Ginsburg's admitted marijuana smoking, NPR played a game of softball that might have embarrassed reporters for 1970s-era *Pravda* when it came to the allegations of sexual misconduct against President Bill Clinton. Daniel Schorr, senior news analyst, gave the First Family this belated Christmas gift on December 26, 1993: "Now, here are the Clintons appearing in Christmas-tide magazine photos as a model, happy family on top of the world. But against the background drumbeat of unseasonable and unpalatable allegations about their private lives. What do you have here? A couple of Arkansas state troopers out for a book and a buck? And Arkansas lawyers who have been gunning for the Clintons? Eleven thousand words in an ultraconservative magazine by David Brock, who did a job on Anita Hill. Surely I don't have to deal with that."[37]

When Arkansas state clerical worker Paula Jones accused Bill Clinton of having harassed her in a manner that made Anita Hill's allegations against Clarence Thomas seem the actions of a Chesterfieldian gentleman, Nina Totenberg was rather rougher on her than she had been on Anita Hill, noting that Jones "was interested in money."[38] In fact, Paula Jones did get money out of this, a *lot* of money, when in 1998 President Clinton paid her $850,000 to drop the lawsuit.[39]

And when in 1993 Totenberg's good friend Ruth Bader Ginsburg was nominated to the U.S. Supreme Court by President Clinton, her treatment of the nominee was generously described as "genteel." Thus was answered the question posed by Reagan administration Justice Department spokesman Terry Eastland, who said as the Clinton administration settled in: "To some extent NPR and Nina are viewed as the perfect outlet if you have dirt on a Republican nominee. Which is not to say that Nina doesn't check it out to make sure that it's good dirt. But it will be very interesting to see if she is as probing with a Democratic administration." Or as Senator Orrin Hatch (R-UT) joked, "Nina? A liberal? *No-oh-oh*! Not Nina. I think Nina makes a legitimate effort to be fair and unbiased, and, of course, fails miserably."[40]

Totenberg's abrasiveness to those below her in the pecking order and her syco-phancy toward powerful people of kindred political bent perhaps accounted for her unpopularity within and without NPR. She "loves to throw her weight around," according to one editor. From various points on the spectrum, she has been described as a "nasty little red baiter" and the "wicked witch of the left," a "self-absorbed nightmare" and "a person with no moral compass."

When Gay Jervey profiled her for *The American Lawyer*, she described her inter-action with a member of the working class: "'It's Miss Totenberg, isn't it'" asks the starstruck cab driver. The star 'mutter[s] that this happens all the time and she really isn't paying these people to recognize her.'" No, she wasn't, but those people are paying a portion of her salary, and perhaps a smidgen of gratitude rather than superciliousness would be in order.[41]

In the 1990s, Totenberg, congressional correspondent and political reporter Cokie Roberts, and *ATC* host Linda Wertheimer, known sexistly as the "fallopian trio," firmly fixed NPR's reputation as the tax-funded bastion of establishment liberalism.[42] Each was one-half of a liberal power couple in the capital: Totenberg with her first husband, Senator Floyd Haskell, a liberal Democrat from Colorado; Wertheimer with her husband, Fred Wertheimer, president of the reformist liberal lobby Common Cause; and the preternaturally connected Roberts, whose husband, Steven, covered Congress and the White House for the *New York Times*, and whose parents, Hale and Lindy Boggs, had been liberal Democratic members of Congress representing New Orleans. Roberts was also a fixture on ABC's *World News Tonight* and *This Week with David Brinkley*, while Totenberg frequently appeared on PBS's *MacNeil/Lehrer News Hour*. But this was hardly the extent of NPR's cross-pollination with the DC establishment. NPR news director Barbara Cohen's husband, Richard Cohen, was a *Washington Post* columnist of liberal bent. (Barbara Cohen, according to former *All*

Things Considered editor Jim Angle, acknowledged the anti-conservative bias in the newsroom, telling him, "There's a real problem in balance and fairness."[43]).

The lineup was so uniform, so one-note, that it gave homogeneity a bad name. It was upper-middle-class white liberalism to the *n*th degree. When NPR took on a black host, Tavis Smiley, he admitted that over those airwaves "I have to be authentically black, but not too black."[44] His hour-long *Tavis Smiley Show* lasted from 2002 to 2004, as programmers and audiences never really warmed up to the mix of news and opinion, often on matters racial. Only 8% of NPR stations even carried Smiley, and a mere handful ran the show during the desired morning drive time.[45]

Though the knowledgeable Cokie Roberts seemed to get along with folks on both sides of the aisle, her reportage was, perhaps unconsciously, liberal-leaning. For instance, when President Clinton's economic stimulus package of 1993 ran into fierce opposition in the House of Representatives, Roberts reported, without bothering to adduce evidence, that there was "more than a little racism" in the fiscally conservative position.[46]

The wickedly humorous leftist columnist Alexander Cockburn of *The Nation* had great fun poking at the puffed-up and oh-so-serious personages of public broad-casting. His eulogy upon Robin MacNeil's departure from *The MacNeil/Lehrer NewsHour* in 1995 was classic. Cockburn needled MacNeil over the fact that over one-quarter (27%) of the funding of *The MacNeil/Lehrer NewsHour* ($6.867 million annually) came from Archer-Daniels Midland, the agribusiness giant which the Cato Institute has called "America's biggest welfare recipient," as 43% of its annual profits then derived from "government subsidies or protection." "Tedium was the very essence" of the *NewsHour*, said Cockburn, as views deviating to any appre-ciable degree from the mainstream were seldom if ever heard. Cockburn concluded: "Lehrer says MacNeil will not be replaced, because he is inimitable. True. Who else could manage that audiovisual equivalent of soup being stirred on a foggy day in the Scottish highlands, that worried frown and instinctive flinch whenever the conversa-tion got interesting, those frantic barks of 'Well, we're nearly out of time' whenever something controversial was on the verge of being uttered? Twenty long, long years of banality. Good night, Robin."[47]

Though NPR was treasured as the jewel in the media crown by establishment liberals, especially those grouped around Washington DC, those further to the left, or less tethered to the establishment, expressed considerable dissatisfaction. Garrison Keillor, in a 1997 interview with leftist David Barsamian over the Boulder, Colorado-based Alternative Radio, complained that NPR was not just too soft on Republicans but also too unaware of them. "Radio has a real obligation here," said the founder of *Prairie Home Companion*, "and I think that *All Things Considered* has seri-ously failed this obligation in recent years. I think the program has for one thing utterly failed to report on the Republican revolution that took control of Congress that has absolutely turned politics upside down in this country. This is not a minor phenomenon. I don't know if reporters at NPR simply don't know Republicans, or they don't know how to talk to them, or what. But this is a crucial story. It goes on under their noses. To ignore that and to do little audio documentaries about old ballplayers and celebrate Paul Robeson's birthday and do a documentary on maple syruping in Vermont is just perverse."[48] (Ironically, Keillor's Minnesota-flavored show was often set up as the antithesis of the Washington-centered hard news approach that NPR's Beltway hands favored.)

Charlotte Ryan, in an extensive 1993 study for the left-wing media watchdog FAIR, found that "NPR's regular coverage mirrored that of commercial news programming: NPR stories focused on the same Washington-centered events and public figures as the commercial news, with the White House and Congress setting much of the agenda." Although its fundraisers sniffily urged listeners to tune in so as to "get the facts as you really can't get them on commercial television," the content of NPR and PBS news reportage had become almost indistinguishable from the staid liberalism of the three major networks. Reviewing transcripts of *All Things Considered* and *Morning Edition* from every weekday between September and December 1991, which included 2296 stories and 5507 persons quoted, Ryan calculated that a plurality (26%) of interviewees were government officials; 22% were journalists, writers, and academics; another 15% were other professionals (lawyers, scientists, and political consultants, for example); and just 10% were ordinary folks—young people, seniors, workers, and other man-or-woman-on-the-street types.

Those journalists who were interviewed by NPR came overwhelmingly from "solidly establishment"—a non-leftist might say "liberal"—outlets: in order, the *Washington Post*, the *New York Times*, the Associated Press, the BBC, and *Newsweek*. As Ryan wrote, "NPR tends to interview those in positions of power, whether in government or in established institutions. The price NPR pays for this conventional approach is that it frequently excludes independent or non-establishment points of view—even on occasions when those views represent a critical mass of the public." She urged NPR to "cast a critical eye on those in power," but this is devilishly difficult to do when you are funded by those in power. Not biting the hand that feeds you is an aphorism of real staying power. An NPR that regularly interviewed outsiders or radicals—say, ardent Trump supporters, pacifists, American Indian radicals, black nationalists, anti-feminist women: people who just do not exist within the range of vision of the mainstream media—would find itself excoriated by those mainstream outlets that currently rush to the defense of NPR when it is criticized by congressional Republicans.

Ryan's study confirmed that the localism that some of NPR's founders envisioned as a linchpin of its operations was about as prominent as stories featuring steelworkers or housewives. Three-fifths, or 59%, of those stories that had a geographic location were based in the Northeast corner of the United States, stretching from the nation's capital to New England. Of these, almost half came out of Washington DC, and more than half of those contained a lead quote by a government official. A name change to BPR—Beltway Public Radio—would more accurately describe the network's focus. A media entity created by the federal government reports on the federal government from a perspective informed disproportionately by employees of that federal government. To expect a fresh and skeptical and independent stance therefrom is to mark oneself as exceptionally credulous.

Although more than a quarter of the American people live in the Midwest, just 10% of the stories were from the vast middle of the country. As for the Rocky Mountains, the Deep South, the Upper Midwest…they were mere afterthoughts.[49]

William E. Buzenberg, vice president for news and information at NPR in Washington from 1990 to 1997, boasted of NPR's nationalizing reach. Unlike in the bad old days of the early '70s, when NPR produced only a single 90-min program which was carried by fewer than 100 stations, by the 1990s NPR was ubiquitous, inescapable. It had transcended the old localism. No matter whether listeners lived "in Missoula, Montana, or New York or Tulsa," they were "linked by interests instead of geography."[50] Local accents, local concerns, local idiosyncrasies, the idea that people in Missoula or Tulsa might have different interests than those in New York: these were yesteryear's beliefs. National Public Radio was doing its best to homogenize its listenership, to focus their attention on the same narrow band of issues that obsessed the staff in Washington DC.

The days of cowboy music and Mardi Gras reveling, of the so-called "Movies of the Air" of the early public radio experimenters, was fast fading.[51] Respectability within the Beltway, which meant the acceptance of conventional Beltway notions of what constituted news and what were the proper bounds delimiting acceptable opinion, was pursued with humorless avidity.

Alan G. Stavitsky has described the changing conception of localism in public broadcasting. Whereas earlier advocates conceived of it in geographic or spatial terms, some intellectuals, who don't bother to hide their contempt for "the mythic haze of the small-town Jeffersonian town square"—they are, one suspects, urban despisers of those unlettered Americans whom they regard as deplorables—are attempting to redefine localism in public radio "in terms of shared interests, tastes, and values." These shared interests, tastes, and values are said to transcend place; they are common to the educated upper-middle-class who make up the bulk of public radio's listenership. Stavitsky instances the issues of "the labor movement, environmental protection, and gay rights"; the idea that there may be multiple sides to these issues is likely not part of this reconceptualized, de-localized localism.[52]

Notes of Chapter

1. Garvin, "How Do I Loathe NPR? Let Me Count the Ways," *Liberty*: 42.
2. Josephson, editor, *Telling the Story: The National Public Radio Guide to Radio Journalism*, p. 9.
3. Jonathan Kern, *Sound Reporting: The NPR Guide to Audio Journalism and Production* (Chicago: University of Chicago Press, 2008), p. 9.
4. Benjamin Hart, "Ventriloquist Journalism at National Public Radio," *Policy Review* (Spring 1984): 76.
5. "National Public Radio Out of Tune," *AIM Report*, May 1985.
6. Hart, "Ventriloquist Journalism at National Public Radio," *Policy Review*: 78.
7. For a skeptical look at conservative claims of bias on the part of PBS, see David Croteau, William Hoynes, and Kevin M. Carragee, "The Political Diversity of Public Television: Polysemy, the Public Square, and the Conservative Critique

of PBS," *Journalism and Mass Communications Monographs*, Vol. 157 (June 1, 1996): 1–55.

8.   Fox, "NPR Grows Up," *American Journalism Review*.
9.   Mitchell, *Listener Supported: The Culture and History of Public Radio*, p. 167.
10. McCauley, *NPR: The Trials and Triumphs of National Public Radio*, p. 112.
11. Fred Barnes, "All Things Distorted," *The New Republic* (October 27, 1986): 17–19.
12. Mitchell, *Listener Supported: The Culture and History of Public Radio*, p. 168.
13. David Boaz, "Ending Taxpayer Funding for Public Broadcasting," Testimony before the Subcommittee on Labor, Health and Human Services, Education, and Related Agencies, Senate Appropriations Committee, July 11, 2005.
14. Huber, "The Static at National Public Radio," Heritage Foundation.
15. Mary S. Larson, "Presidential News Coverage and 'All Things Considered': National Public Radio and News Bias," *Presidential Studies Quarterly*, Vol. 19, No. 2 (Spring 1989): 350–51.
16. Ibid.: 352.
17. Clark, "Public Broadcasting," *CQ Researcher*: 3.
18. Zansberg, "'Objectivity and Balance' in Public Broadcasting: Unwise, Unworkable, and Unconstitutional," *Yale Law & Policy Review*: 225.
19. Garvin, "How Do I Loathe NPR? Let Me Count the Ways," *Liberty*: 40.
20. Clark, "Public Broadcasting," *CQ Researcher*: 9.
21. Zansberg, "'Objectivity and Balance' in Public Broadcasting: Unwise, Unworkable, and Unconstitutional," *Yale Law & Policy Review*: 185–86. See also Howard A. White, "Fine Tuning the Federal Government's Role in Public Broadcasting," *Federal Communications Law Journal*, Vol. 46 (1994): 501–514.
22. Zansberg, "'Objectivity and Balance' in Public Broadcasting: Unwise, Unworkable, and Unconstitutional," *Yale Law & Policy Review*: 201.
23. Ibid.: 187.
24. Ibid.: 194.
25. Husseini, "The Broken Promise of Public Radio," *The Humanist*: 127.
26. "The 1992 Republican Platform," adopted August 17, 1992, www.cnn.com, accessed September 12, 2019.
27. *This is NPR: The First Forty Years*, p. 150.
28. Barsamian, *The Decline and Fall of Public Broadcasting*, pp. 33–34.
29. "Letter from an Anonymous NPR Producer," in *Public Broadcasting and the Public Trust*, pp. 174–175.
30. Ibid., p. 174.
31. Ibid., p. 176.
32. Gregory Elson, "When Reporters Make News," *Time* (October 28, 1991).
33. Dennis McDougal, "Reporter Takes Heat on Ginsburg: Totenberg Says She Used Marijuana Once," *Los Angeles Times*, November 12, 1987.
34. John Hockenberry, *Moving Violations: War Zones, Wheelchairs, and Declarations of Independence* (New York: Hyperion, 1995), pp. 174, 177.
35. Ibid., pp. 177–78.

36.   Gay Jervey, "Diva Nina," *The American Lawyer* (November 1993).
37.   *Public Broadcasting and the Public Trust*, p. 205.
38.   Ibid., p. 210.
39.   Peter Baker, "Clinton Settles Paula Jones Lawsuit for $850,000." *Washington Post*, November 14, 1998.
40.   Jervey, "Diva Nina," *The American Lawyer*.
41.   Ibid.
42.   Porter, "Has Success Spoiled NPR?" *Columbia Journalism Review*: 28.
43.   Fox, "NPR Grows Up," *American Journalism Review*.
44.   Montopoli, "All Things Considerate," *Washington Monthly*.
45.   McCauley, *NPR: The Trials and Triumphs of National Public Radio*, p. 125.
46.   Garvin, "How Do I Loathe NPR? Let Me Count the Ways," *Liberty*: 40.
47.   Alexander Cockburn, "Beat the Devil," *The Nation* (November 13, 1995).
48.   Barsamian, *The Decline and Fall of Public Broadcasting*, p. 20.
49.   Charlotte Ryan, "A Study of National Public Radio," FAIR, www.fair.org, April 1, 1993.
50.   William E. Buzenberg, "Growing NPR," in *Radio: The Forgotten Medium*, p. 181.
51.   Porter, "Has Success Spoiled NPR?" *Columbia Journalism Review*: 27.
52.   Alan G. Stavitsky, "The Changing Conception of Localism in U.S. Public Radio," *Journal of Broadcasting & Electronic Media* (Winter 1994): 27, 19.

Chapter 7
Newt [Gingrich] Cometh

The interval between the historic November 1994 congressional elections, when a Republican insurgency led by future Speaker Newt Gingrich (R-GA) ended 38 years of Democratic rule in the U.S. House of Representatives, and the assumption of power by those Republicans in January 1995, saw furious lobbying by NPR officials, though they disdained so sordid a word as *lobbying*. That's what burly union officials and slick corporate types do. They preferred "grass roots campaign," which assumes that phone calls from NPR station managers, visits to Capitol Hill by NPR celebrity journalists, and urgent communications from the influential personages who typically constitute the board of directors of an NPR station emerge from the grass roots.[1]

Newt Gingrich had announced on his National Empowerment Network weekly television program his plan to "zero-out CPB, which has been eating taxpayers' money." He said that taxpayers were "involuntarily" subsidizing biased reporting.[2] Moreover, he charged, it was a regressive arrangement through which ordinary taxpayers had to subsidize the entertainment choices of "rich, upper-class people."[3] If tractor pulls and country music shows had to make it in the market, why not middle-brow radio and television shows for people who looked down upon tractor pulls and country music? The new Speaker of the House told the audience at a Capitol Hill luncheon: "I don't understand why they call it public broadcasting. As far as I'm concerned there's nothing public about it. It's an elitist enterprise. Rush Limbaugh is public broadcasting."[4]

Over in the self-declared world's greatest deliberative body, Senator Larry Pressler (R-SD), incoming chairman of the Senate Commerce Committee, was using the P-word: *privatization*.[5] "Large corporations are lined up to advertise on public radio and television," said Senator Pressler, to the dismay of purists and those who enjoyed the periodic fundraisers.[6] "There are millions of dollars being made on *Barney* and *Sesame Street* and on the *Civil War* series and Louis Rukeyser," said Senator Pressler, referencing PBS's greatest hits. "I want to see CPB get a portion of the profits. Then you could zero it out and you wouldn't need taxpayer funds."[7] (NPR, as its then-president Delano Lewis protested, had no equivalent to the cash cow that is *Sesame Street*.[8]) Despite the frequent expostulations by its defenders that the CPB,

© The Author(s), under exclusive license to Springer Nature Switzerland AG 2021   99
J. T. Bennett, *The History and Politics of Public Radio*, Studies in Public Choice 41,
https://doi.org/10.1007/978-3-030-80019-2_7

and especially NPR, receive just a minority—even a small minority—of funding from the federal treasury, PBS president Ervin Duggan said in response to Pressler's initiative that privatization was akin to "assisted suicide."[9]

The coverage of Senator Pressler's campaign to privatize the CPB provides a nice illustration of the way that ideological bias determines what different news organizations judge to be news and not news. In the same week of February 1995, the *Washington Post*, reliably liberal, and the upstart *Washington Times*, reliably conservative, ran stories about Pressler.

The *Post* story took what might charitably be described as a skeptical angle. Senator Pressler had compiled 168 questions from what he said were "minority groups, religious groups, Jewish groups, Christian groups," and others into a sixteen-page questionnaire which he sent to CPB in late January 1995. Corporation spokespeople, obviously acting as sources for *Post* reporter Ellen Edwards, told her that answering the questions took "an estimated 1800 man-hours" at a cost of $92,000, of which $15,000 was paid to two law firms, Skadden, Arps, Slate, Meagher & Flom, and the more euphonious Covington & Burling, which vetted the thousands of pages submitted as answers to Senator Pressler's questions "to make sure that no proprietary information was being revealed about people or businesses with which CPB has contracts."[10]

The thrust of the story was a mocking treatment of Pressler, an ostensible budget-cutter who was making the poor overworked public servants of CPB (and the aspiring young partners at prestigious DC law firms) toil into the wee hours of the night digging up snappy answers to stupid questions, to borrow the old *Mad Magazine* formula. Whether or not any of these questions had been worth asking was left unexplored. That same week, George Archibald filed a page-one story at the *Washington Times* centered on an analysis by Senator Pressler's Commerce Committee of the federal subsidies other than direct appropriations that are granted to public broadcasting. While CPB's then-current annual appropriation was $285.6 million, the monopoly broadcast licenses granted to PBS stations alone exceeded $5 billion in value, and federal monies doled out to purchase equipment and facilities for public radio and television stations were estimated to have exceeded $500 million under the Public Telecommunications Facilities program. The headline indicated the tilt of the *Times*: "Public broadcasting's federal subsidy far exceeds appropriation."[11] There was no mention of the 168 questions Senator Pressler had posed to the CPB, nor the cost incurred in ginning up answers thereto.

Richard Carlson, president of CPB—and father of future Fox News star Tucker Carlson—expressed confidence that the Corporation's champions could convincingly defend federal funding to skeptical Republicans, though he conciliatingly conceded that this would be a good time for "public TV and radio to get its house in order. To correct its mistakes, to make sure it's not wasting public money, and to make sure its *programs* are fair and balanced."[12] (In this last hope he anticipated his son's employer, Fox News, which would later adopt "fair and balanced" as its motto.)

NPR President Delano Lewis warned that smaller stations, presumably in rural and Republican areas, might have to close up shop if federal aid were withdrawn. Lewis, as seems to be par for the course for NPR presidents, came from a Democratic political background, specifically his involvement with Washington DC, Mayor Marion Barry, and DC congressional delegate Walter Fauntroy. "I do not want to privatize," Lewis told a House Appropriations subcommittee in January 1995, as the newly ascendant House Republicans cast a skeptical eye on a news organization which not even its supporters could claim with a straight face offered sympathetic or understanding coverage of issues close to Republican hearts. But mindful of the new political landscape, he said, "I'm not dismissing ideas."[13] As the Gingrich Republicans cast a jaundiced eye upon public broadcasting, Lewis predicted that at some unspecified time in the relatively near future his organization would find, or devise, "a whole new source of funds that would not be from the taxpayers directly." This might be in the form of an endowment, a trust fund, spectrum fees, or perhaps a genie emerging from a bottle. For the then-present, however, Lewis lobbied hard against GOP plans to reduce the Corporation for Public Broadcasting's budget by up to 30%.[14]

The elite media reached into the storehouse of public broadcasting stock characters for their stories on Gingrich the ogre. Karen De Witt, writing in the *New York Times*, typed out what was virtually a boilerplate lede: "If incoming Speaker Newt Gingrich has his way, Barney and Big Bird and *All Things Considered* and *Morning Edition* will disappear from the publicly financed airwaves permanently." (An earnest -- or cynical --over-the-air fundraiser for your local NPR or PBS station would have phrased it exactly the same way.) De Witt went on to quote various defenders of CPB, both academic and institutional. CPB president Richard Carlson gamely suggested that his corporation was "a good deal for the taxpayer," who pitches in "about a buck per person" per year.[15]

Judy Mann, a *Washington Post* columnist, quoted a Republican strategist named Steve Hofman claiming that the effort to defund CPB was a political move to make other spending cuts more palatable. There was, said Hofman, "a firm belief on the Republican side that if you can't address elite subsidies, then you're not going to have any legitimacy to do much else on the spending side of the budget." The "basic premise," he said, "is if you've got to start somewhere, the elite subsidies are a pretty good place to start, when the bulk of the taxes are paid by middle-class Americans and the bulk of the debt is going to be carried by their children." In Pavlovian fashion, Mann flew straight to Big Bird: "I'm having trouble thinking of the millions of toddlers who watch *Sesame Street* as elites-in-training." This willful obtuseness is standard in mainstream columnizing about threats to the Corporation for Public Broadcasting. The abundant research on the demographics of NPR and PBS consumers—much of it brandished by CPB executives in search of corporate under-writers—Mann of course leaves blissfully unvisited, lest it disturb the mandatory *Sesame Street* reference.

Mann does, however, concede that the claim by CPB that federal monies account for just 3% of NPR's budget gainsays the dire consequences predicted by its defenders in the event of defunding. She goes on to suggest, no doubt to the dismay of the NPR execs reading their morning paper, that perhaps public broadcasting should be funded by a $1 checkoff on IRS forms, as was done (to widespread indifference and declining participation, it should be noted) with presidential campaign financing.

This would provide a "marketplace incentive to deliver programs with broad appeal and continued balance [*sic*]." What's more, decoupling the CPB from the federal treasury would free NPR and PBS to become "a genuinely liberal alternative to the conservative ideology now spreading through the commercial airwaves" in the person of Rush Limbaugh and his epigoni.[16]

Such a development would be perfectly unobjectionable; an intelligent radio counterpart to CNN or MSNBC, while perhaps doing little to elevate public discussion, would find an audience, and if it retained the residual qualities that once made NPR different—its ear occasionally cocked to happenings outside the Beltway or the Acela Corridor—it might be worth a listen.

Mann's scornful reference to the right-wing radio ranters raises the question of why, by the 1990s and early 2000s, talk radio had become so overwhelmingly conservative. This was not the doing of some nefarious right-wing plot to force the unwary into listening to Rush Limbaugh, Sean Hannity, Dr. Laura Schlessinger, and numerous local hosts. Their success was a product of the marketplace of ideas and entertainment; it also points to the huge demand for non-liberal radio that was not being met by commercial or, especially, public radio. As William G. Mayer wrote in *The Public Interest*, liberals "do not need talk radio: They have…. NPR."[17] (The liberal riposte to this was that "[i]n the sea of vituperative right-wing radio, NPR is an island of sanity, civility, and seriousness."[18]).

Liberals had sought to counterprogram the Limbaughs with their own hosts, but in the 1990s eminences such as Mario Cuomo, Alan Dershowitz, and Gary Hart had flamed out quickly in the attempt, and the early 21st-century left-of-center Air America network likewise fizzled. A survey in 2003, near the height of the talk radio phenomenon, found that 11 of the 28 top radio talk programs were "hosted by outspoken, undisguised conservatives," while not a single one was hosted by someone "clearly and unambiguously liberal."

The blame, for those who believe the situation called out for blame, rested with audiences, not a cabal of right-wing program directors. According to William Mayer, when Colin McEnroe, liberal host of a talk show on WTIC in Hartford, Connecticut, was canned, he at first thought himself a victim of the conservative wave in radio. But he soon learned the truth: "It turned out my bosses' politics weren't that different from mine. All they cared about was the ratings. If Noam Chomsky playing the kazoo on air got them an 11 share, they would put him on."[19]

Half a year into his Speakership, Gingrich had backed off. "Big Bird Taken Off Death Row," read the predictable headline in the *Washington Post*. The famously irrepressible Speaker sounded apologetic: "If I had to go back and redo the last months, I would enter the PBS debate totally differently," he said on a PBS program, that of the later-to-be-#MeToo-ed Charlie Rose. "This is not a system that has to stay on the taxpayers' back, but we do want to keep a public broadcasting system. And I think that I—I think by emphasizing the cut-half of that conversation, I sent exactly the wrong signal." As if he were referring to Yosemite or the Washington Monument rather than *Washington Week* he stressed, "I think the federal government should keep federal assets."[20]

The Republican threat to starve the CPB was as empty as most political oratory. In March 1995, as Republicans were crowing over their new majority, Rep. Phil Crane (R-IL) proposed an amendment on the House floor that would have reduced CPB funding by one-third in FY 1996, two-thirds in FY 1997, and completely in FY 1998. This is, more or less, what party rhetoricians had pledged, but Crane's amendment was routed by a vote of 350–72.[21] Other Republicans spoke of gradual phase-outs or modest reductions, but such reductions turned out to be largely illusory, and the cuts superficial, or at least eminently survivable.

Minor reductions in the CPB appropriations paled beside those doled out to the Departments of Labor and Education. Senator Pressler kept insisting that "a three-year phaseout is realistic," but his vision of a system propped up by *Sesame Street* swag sales and Ken Burns's grandiloquently epic histories and underwriting from prestige corporations seeking to please affluent consumers quickly dimmed. In the summer of 1995, a House Appropriations Subcommittee on Labor, Health and Human Services, Education, and Related Agencies rejected by a single vote a motion by Rep. Dan Miller (R-FL) to end CPB funding by FY 1998: the corporation was saved when moderate Illinois Republican John Porter, the subcommittee chairman, joined the Democrats in opposition to Miller's motion. Rep. Porter claimed to support an eventual phase-out of federal funding, but that eventuality was far down the road, well beyond the end of Rep. Porter's career in January 2001. David Brugger, president of America's Public Television Stations, the PBS lobbying group, told the *Washington Post* that public broadcasting was on "a glide path to zero" sometime after 2002—but that, too, is nowhere in sight, and it far exceeds the length of Brugger's stint at APTS, which ended at about the same time as Rep. Porter left Congress.[22]

For all the huffing and puffing and sky-is-falling imagery, the congressional appropriation for the Corporation for Public Broadcasting (see Table 7.1), which had been $285.6 million in fiscal year 1995, the last fiscal year before the advent of Speaker Gingrich, dipped to $275 million in FY 1996, $260 million in FY 1997, and $250 million in FY 1998 and 1999 before rebounding to $300 million FY 2000, and reaching $400 million by the end of the presidency of President George W. Bush.

The minatory specter of Newt Gingrich proved a fund-raising bonanza for NPR, just as the likes of such polarizing political figures as Senators Jesse Helms (R-NC) and Ted Kennedy (D-MA) had helped direct-mail mavens raise untold millions through boogeyman solicitation letters mailed to politically interested Americans. Reagan had served a similar role for liberals and Democrats in the early 1980s. For instance, in 1982, Wisconsin Public Radio ran a "Seven Days in May" fundraiser that brought in "far more money" than expected.[23] The title was borrowed from Fletcher Knebel and Charles Bailey's political novel about a right-wing coup and was obviously targeted at the sort of liberal who worried that "Ronnie Ray-Gun" was going to bring about fascism in the USA. The same tactic was employed at Pacifica. As a former KPFK staffer told Jesse Walker, "Newt Gingrich was not a threat. Pacifica was poised to profit greatly off of Newt Gingrich. All you had to do was be there and basically say, 'We criticized Gingrich.' And the money would come in."[24]

Table 7.1 Corporation for Public Broadcasting federal appropriation fiscal years 1969–2020 ($ millions)

FY	$	FY	$	FY	$
1969	5	1987	200	2005	387
1970	15	1988	214	2006	396
1971	23	1989	228	2007	400
1972	35	1990	229	2008	393
1973	35	1991	299	2009	400
1974	50	1992	327	2010	420
1975	62[a]	1993	319	2011	429
1976	79	1994	275	2012	444
1977	103	1995	286	2013	422
1978	119	1996	275	2014	445
1979	120	1997	260	2015	445
1980	152	1998	250	2016	445
1981	162	1999	250	2017	445
1982	172	2000	300	2018	445
1983	137	2001	340	2019	445
1984	138	2002	350	2020	445
1985	151	2003	363		
1986	160	2004	378		

Source Glenn J. McLoughlin and Lena A. Gomez, "The Corporation for Public Broadcasting: Federal Funding and Issues," Congressional Research Service, May 3, 2017, pp. 3–5
Note [a]with 17.5 in the Transition Quarter from July–September as the federal budget year changed

Now that Pacifica was accepting funds from the CPB, it drifted back into the crosshairs of the Right. The Reaganites called it "Radio Sandinista," for its open sympathy with the leftist government of Nicaragua.[25] Fierce internecine battles broke out with some regularity, sometimes pitting the board of directors against the staff. There were battles with external forces, too: the Houston station's transmitter was twice bombed in the late 1960s by, presumably, radicals of the Right.[26]

Pacifica, despite its beginnings in pacifism and voluntary support, was by the 1980s and 1990s regarded as "urban" and "left-wing."[27] Diversity, by then a corporate buzzword, meant uniformity in practice at Pacifica. When William Barlow studied community radio in the late 1980s, he noted that the putatively alternative stations "share the same broadly defined ideological orientation," by which he meant the championship of "progressive politics, alternative cultures, and participatory democracy," though three decades later, that commitment to democracy seemed rather shaky when it came to accepting the verdict of the voters and the Electoral College in the election of Donald Trump.[28] The legitimacy of democratic elections, it appears, depends upon whether the choice made by the people is consonant with the preferences of those who run the radio stations.

Victor Gold, a long-time Republican Party activist and consultant who had served as the feisty press secretary to Vice President Spiro Agnew and adviser to the first President Bush, was appointed to the board of the Corporation for Public Broadcasting by that same President Bush. In 1993, he called for defunding Pacifica and other stations that, in his words, "repeatedly sponsor and air anti-Semitic, racist, and other hate programs."[29] Gold's ire had been piqued by a series of events culminating with "African Mental Liberation Weekend" in February 1993. Professor Leonard Jeffries, the long-time chairman of the City College of New York's Black Studies Department who was frequently criticized for allegedly anti-Semitic remarks in the 1990s, was a featured guest; the previous year's African Mental Liberation Weekend had included a speech by Louis Farrakan, leader of the Nation of Islam, who had also been under consistent fire for remarks that certainly seemed both anti-Semitic and anti-white. Gold, noting that KPFK-FM had taken in $365,115 in Community Service Grants from the CPB in 1992–1993, asked why taxpayers should have to shell out for a "persistent pattern of anti-Semitic programming." He was not, he hastened to add, calling for censorship, but rather for the cessation of federal subsidy of what he termed "hate broadcasting." The CPB board rejected Gold's proposal, sending the famously short-tempered Gold into orbit. He blasted his fellow board members for being "hypocritical and disingenuous."[30] Senator Bob Dole, eyeing a 1996 presidential campaign and seeking to shore up his credentials with the Right, picked up the banner from Gold and threatened congressional reprisal against Pacifica. "The First Amendment, freedom of speech, doesn't apply," said Dole, "because we are able to put conditions on the grants of federal money. The same as we do for farmers."[31] Dole's effort fell short; CPB and Pacifica remained under the federal spigot.

Pacifica was no longer the collection of freewheeling anarchist stations of yore; its administration and even programming had become centralized, its stations were into the CPB for upwards of a million dollars a year, and one could listen for days at a time without encountering challenging voices from the right. The atmosphere of political correctness was suffocating. And those endless internecine battles which seemed to pit Stalinist management against subalterns who chafed at dictatorial edicts came close to sinking the network.

The Rich Get Richer

Thomas Looker, author of *The Sound and the Story: NPR and the Art of Radio* (1995), locates NPR's origin in educational radio, which, he says, had a "strongly rural profile" with an audience of "students, farmers, teachers, and small-town professionals." Its roots, Looker argues, "are populist, growing out of the same rural, self-reliant, self-improving soil as the Chautauqua Movement or the Grange."[32]

True, if one goes back far enough, but William Jennings Bryan and his followers are not the desired audience today. Jesse Walker's claim that NPR is, for the most part, "upscale and middlebrow, offering hour after hour of candy-coated brie," is verified by the organization's own proudly advertised data.[33] (The first half of Walker's indictment is verified, that is; NPR would demur at the second half.)

In 2003, an NPR-commissioned study by Mediamark Research discovered—as NPR boasted—that: "Public radio listeners are driven to learn more, to earn more, to spend more, and to be more involved in their communities. They are leaders and decision makers, both in the boardroom and in the town square. They are more likely to exert their influence on their communities in all types of ways—from voting to volunteering." And that's not all: "Public radio listeners are dynamic—they do more. They are much more likely than the general public to travel to foreign nations, to attend concerts and art events, and to exercise regularly. They are health conscious, and are less likely to have serious health problems. Their media usage patterns reflect their active lifestyles, they tend to favor portable media such as newspapers or radio."

The payoff to potential advertisers, or underwriters, as the euphemism goes, is this: "As consumers, they are more likely to have a taste for products that deliver on the promise of quality. Naturally, they tend to spend more on products and services." Compared to the general public—that is, those middle-manager Rush Limbaugh listeners, or the guys in the stockroom talking about NASCAR, or the clerk and cashier who take care of your grocery needs—NPR listeners circa 2003, according to the Mediamark study, were:

- 55% less likely to have a household income below $30,000
- 117% more likely to have a household income above $150,000
- 152% more likely to have a home valued at $500,000 or more
- 194% more likely to travel to France
- 326% more likely to read the *New Yorker*
- 125% more likely to own bonds
- 125% more likely to own a Volvo.[34]

In what hall-of-mirrors world does such a demographic deserve having its radio listening habits subsidized?

No wonder, says David Boaz when considering those demographics, that "you hear ads for Remy Martin and 'private banking services' on NPR, not for Budweiser and free checking accounts."[35] Its gold-plated listenership endows NPR sponsors with the desired cachet, which of course is the reason this research is brandished by the sales force. In its annual report of 1992, NPR's flacks boasted that when one corporate representative revealed to others at a swanky gathering that his company underwrote public radio, "it was as if I was suddenly a representative of Mother Teresa."[36]

Chasing corporate and foundation contributions is not without a downside, in the view of some friendly critics. Wilbur Mills understood that there are always strings attached when government doles out tax monies, and internal NPR critics have groused that the acceptance of corporate and foundation support has also entailed strings. In 1990, Richard Salant, formerly president of CBS News, resigned as a director of NPR in protest of its acceptance of grants for coverage of specific issues. For instance, at the time of Salant's resignation the Lilly Endowment's subvention to NPR was dedicated to the coverage of issues affecting children; this coverage, one may be sure, was slanted in a direction congenial to Lilly.

NPR Managing Editor John Dinges told Nicols Fox of the *American Journalism Review* that while he "would prefer money with absolutely no strings attached," the great danger was not so much out and out bias as it was the degree of coverage an issue might get. Grants encourage NPR to cover some issues "more extensively than we would have if left to our own devices. Sometimes I think we're a bit skewed in our overall mix of coverage."[37] And as former CPB director Howard Husock notes, the choice of which stories to cover is often the real index of bias. For instance, in 2016–2017 NPR covered in full the protests over the Dakota Access Pipeline but disdained to cover "the economic benefits of fracking."[38]

The gift to dwarf all gifts was gifted in 2003, when Joan Kroc, widow of McDonald's hamburger titan Ray Kroc—"that's Kroc with a K/like crocodile but not spelled that way," as Mark Knopfler sang in "Boom Like That"—left NPR a bequest of $222 million, which was, at the time, "the largest gift that had ever been given to a cultural organization."[39] It was about twice the size of NPR's portion of the CPB annual budgets in the early twenty-first century, and enabled NPR to boost its budget by more than 50% in 2004.

(Joan had been a pianist in a St. Paul, Minnesota, restaurant, when Ray Kroc, 26 years her senior and married to boot --as was she --saw her, heard her playing, and fell in love. She returned his interest, though whether or not it was love or a canny jumping at the chance to marry a rich man: who can tell? She dumped her husband, a McDonald's franchisee, and he dumped his second wife, and they married. In her widowhood, Joan lived largely and lavishly, and donated to some groups which were not exactly on Ray's menu.)

Thirteen years after Joan Kroc's gift, Lisa Napoli, author of *Ray And Joan: The Man Who Made The McDonald's Fortune And The Woman Who Gave It All Away*, had this exchange with NPR's Scott Simon:

SIMON: How fair or accurate is the idea that Joan Kroc gave away Ray Kroc's money to a lot of places and causes of which he would not have approved?
NAPOLI: A lot of old-guard McDonald's people I've talked to are angry that Joan made gifts that, in their estimation, were more liberal-leaning than Ray, perhaps, would've liked, including her million-dollar gift to the Democrats ... and her active work in the peace movement and building these peace institutes at both Notre Dame and the University of San Diego.
I don't think she did it to spite Ray or to get back at him at all, although I do know that during the course of their marriage, she said she suppressed her politics and her interests in some ways because she didn't want to seem untoward.[40]

Mediamark did not survey NPR listeners about their fast-food habits, but it is safe to say that the sources of Joan Kroc's fortune have little overlap with the universe of Terry Gross listeners.

Just Pennies a Person!
Given the demographic profile of NPR listeners, their lobbying for additional funding is a vivid example of the rich getting (or trying to get) richer at the expense of the non-rich. The most affluent Americans lobby Congress to use taxpayer funds to

subsidize their favorite programs, thus shifting the burden of support from voluntary private supporters to involuntary and coerced payers of taxes. It is pork for the upper-middle-class, the most highly educated, the people most able to pay for their own cultural excursions and entertainments. In the words of Howard Husock, it is a "niche programming service for a left-leaning, upmarket urban constituency."[41]

The case for NPR being a subsidy of elite tastes is even stronger than the case against PBS. For *Sesame Street* and other children's programming do attract a not insignificant viewership among poorer Americans. (Setting aside the fact that if PBS had disappeared at midnight any time after its most popular children's show went on the air in 1969, *Sesame Street* and its kindred programs would have been picked up by commercial networks or channels at 12:01. In fact, the cable giant HBO bought the rights to first-run *Sesame Street* episodes in 2016, so the Big Bird scare tactic no longer flies.) There is no *Sesame Street* of NPR. Despite Bill Siemering's lucubrations, public radio never really aimed its offerings at children. It is an adults-only project, and the adults it serves are overwhelmingly not black or Hispanic or working-class white or rural. As Sheldon Richman says, "the middle class pays and the upper crust consumes."[42] The audience remains overwhelmingly tilted toward people with higher incomes and higher levels of formal education. Boston, Washington, San Francisco, and college towns were in the 1970s and are today the strongholds of NPR.[43] All those airy notions floated by the pioneers of reaching African Americans, Hispanics, rural people, the poor: they came to nothing.

The radicalism that some conservatives feared would turn NPR into an institutionalized organ of the New Left has never had much purchase; instead, a blander upper-middle-class liberalism has prevailed, leaving other voices, whether left, right, or apolitical, unheard—but not untapped for tax contributions. "It is a monstrous proposition," argued Trevor Burrus, legal associate at the Cato Institute's Center for Constitutional Studies, "to say that already marginalized voices should continue to be marginalized by a state-sponsored institution—that the marginalized should support their own marginalization."[44]

To deflect the potentially potent charge that the CPB's federal support amounted to a regressive transfer of wealth, its defenders took to minimizing the significance of the subsidy. During the Gingrich threat, or perceived threat, the argument went like this: Government support of public broadcasting amounts to $1.06 per American, but $32.15 per Canadian and $38.15 per Brit.[45] That's peanuts! Look how much more onerous the burden is in Canada and Great Britain. The CPB's annual appropriation equals one cup of coffee at your local diner per American, so what's the big deal? Quit yer complainin'.

This claim that the average American loses more money in the sofa cushions than he is taxed each year to support the CPB is hauled out every time the public subsidy is questioned. When in 2019 Donald Trump once again proposed, half-heartedly, to zero out CPB funding, PBS president Paula Kerger cited the "modest investment of about $1.35 per citizen per year."[46] So hey, goes the implication: what's the big deal? Why grumble over such a paltry expenditure?

Arnold Steinberg, who as a 20-year-old student participated in the Public Broadcasting Laboratory, a 1967–1969 Ford Foundation-funded project which is asserted to have been the forerunner of PBS public-affairs programs, argues, "The per capita formulation is the refuge of those who cannot defend the expenditure's constitutionality, morality or wisdom."[47] It is the equivalent of a no-harm, no-foul non-call in basketball, or the criminal justice system dismissing charges against a shoplifter because his take was less than $100 in merchandise. It is no defense; it is merely a slightly embarrassed request to look the other way. Arnold Steinberg's invocation of the CPB's questionable constitutionality rings anachronistically in our era of extreme loose construction. Yet the question raised by libertarian Sheldon Richman in testimony before the Subcommittee on Energy and Mineral Resources of the U.S. House of Representatives (an inapt jurisdictional title) retains, for some, a certain force and relevancy: "Where in Article 1 is the Congress empowered to transfer money from the one group of citizens to another for the purpose of supporting broadcasting?"[48] The answer is that it is not there, and only a broad reading of the implied powers of Congress can so locate it.

The failure of the Republican Party to terminate CPB funding during its years of ascendancy astonished more libertarian-minded observers. The Cato Institute's David Boaz, for instance, said that "it's unbelievable to me that Republicans appropriate money every year for two networks that could be called ARN, the Anti-Republican Network." Instead, he observed, ham-fisted Republican solons try to hector and bully NPR and PBS into promoting conservative causes and celebrities.[49] Their objection seems to be less to the expenditure of federal monies on projects they regard as unconstitutional than it is to the ideological orientation of those projects; were NPR and PBS in the back pockets of the Republican Party, it seems that the GOP's legislative leaders would drop even token opposition to their funding.

During the mild George W. Bush-era Republican dust-up with public broadcasting, both NPR and PBS engaged without apology in blatant lobbying. Public radio and television aired thirty-second announcements asking listeners and viewers to take action to "save public broadcasting." The organizations' websites urged readers, "Please call your Senator today to express your support of federal funding for Public Broadcasting."[50] Thus recipients of federal monies were using at least a portion of those monies to demand the continuance of federal support. It worked; the circle of dependence was unbroken.

PBS documentarian Ken Burns propounded what might be termed the condescending case for public broadcasting when he said, "We ought to be able to allocate a minuscule fraction of our budget for rich intellectual history rather than allow a marketplace to dominate an illiterate country where people know every cast member of *Gilligan's Island* but can't name six presidents." But then an excessive sense of self-importance has been a mark of CPB executives through the years. "We are a self-righteous crowd who believe that what we are doing is essential to democracy itself," crowed PBS president Bruce Christiansen in 1992. At about that same time, as the CPB was easily fending off Senator Dole's attempt to freeze its funding, Virginia G. Fox, executive director of Kentucky public television, said that federal subsidy of her medium would no longer be necessary when "Bob Dole can prove that they've solved the problem of undereducated people"—a group which to Ms. Fox was probably coterminous with those who would vote for Mr. Dole.[51] (The acme of

NPR smugness today is the allegedly comedic show "Wait, Wait...Don't Tell Me!" in which a cadre of unfunny comedians mock Trump, Trump voters, and anyone outside their demographic. As Brian Montopoli wrote in *Washington Monthly*, this "cringe-inducing show" is "an excuse for a group of panelists with a suspicious similarity to their target audience to express their delight and whimsy at how clever and informed they are."[52]).

Not for Conservatives

Conservatives have termed NPR the "taxpayer-funded wing of the Democratic Party," which has evinced "a fetish for hate crimes in the Trump era," often relying on the potted and invidious takes of the discredited Southern Poverty Law Center, a fundraising machine founded by the direct-mail maven Morris Dees. When an unbalanced man stabbed three people in Portland, Oregon, in 2017, the SPLC guest told *All Things Considered* that this was just another example of crazies committing horrid hate crimes against "those populations demonized by the Trump campaign and now Trump administration."[53] Both the SPLC guest and the *All Things Considered* host knew that the murderer was a supporter of Bernie Sanders and Green Party candidate Jill Stein, and that his social media proclamations were decidedly left wing, but, well, why let the facts get in the way of NPR's Narrative?

Senator Sanders, as critic of NPR David Boaz noted, was prominently featured on the *Diane Rehm Show* upon the release of his book *The Speech* in 2011, whereas the author of a contemporaneously released (and much better-selling) book, Rand Paul (*The Tea Party Goes to Washington*), was not.[54] Like the selection of topics, the choice of guests helps to define the news, and to delimit the bounds of acceptable opinion. Ignoring is not the same as censoring, but in some respects, it is even more effective at enfeebling or concealing dissenters.

A long-standing complaint by critics on the Right is that NPR identifies guests or people who are quoted as "conservative" or belonging to "conservative" think tanks or interest groups, but does not do the same for liberals. Ryan Bourne, an economist affiliated with the libertarian (to use an accurate identifier) Cato Institute, examined such bias—what he calls "health warnings," as if listeners or viewers must be cautioned before a right-of-center guest speaks—in BBC broadcasts between 2010 and 2015. He found that the four major free-market think tanks in the UK were slapped with such labels as "free-market," "centre-right," and "right-wing" with some frequency: Adam Smith Institute (59.5%), Policy Exchange (41.7%), Centre for Policy Studies (30.3%), and Institute of Economic Affairs (22.1%).

It's not that these labels are necessarily inaccurate, though they often simplify or, in some cases, obfuscate. But groups on the left side of the policy debate were almost never labeled. For instance, the New Economic Foundation, which Bourne describes as "the most left-leaning policy think tank in the country," was slapped with a health warning just once, and it was not so much a warning as it was a seal of approval. Instead of calling it, as some might, leftist or environmentalist or whatnot, it was deemed an advocate of "sustainability," a warm and fuzzy term.[55] As Bernard Goldberg, a former CBS correspondent, said by way of explaining the disparity in labeling, "Conservatives are out of the mainstream and need to be identified. Liberals, on the other hand, *are* the mainstream and don't need to be identified."[56]

David Boaz notes that the selection of topics dovetails with the point of view to give NPR and PBS an overwhelming lopsidedness. While there are reports aplenty on "racism, sexism, and environmental destruction," one would look long and hard and in vain for stories or documentary accounts of "the burden of taxes, or the number of people who have died because federal regulations kept drugs off the market, or the way that state governments have abused the law in their pursuit of tobacco companies, or the number of people who use guns to prevent crimes."[57] It is in fact inconceivable that NPR would broadcast a story with any of these angles, though of course individuals interviewed might express such sentiments in the interest of the elusive balance that is said to be a desideratum.

Even Jack Mitchell, in his richly informative book of analysis and memoir, *Listener Supported: The Culture and History of Public Radio* (2005), concluded that "Government is a dubious source of funding for an institution designed to question the unquestioned ... Public radio is as unlikely as a dog to bite the hand that feeds it."[58] To give an example, Mark Huber, assessing NPR's political bent in 1985, wrote, "There is little chance that NPR will air a negative story on Representative John Dingell (D-MI), chairman of the House Energy and Commerce Committee, any time soon. Dingell's committee controls NPR funding."[59] That particular hand went unbitten.

Mike Gonzalez, in an essay for the Knight Foundation, conceded that public broadcasting is not in the nature of a government propaganda machine but rather reflects the fairly uniform and establishment outlook of "a *bien pensant* coalition of government bureaucrats, academics, entertainers, philanthropists, ethnic group activists, corporate leaders, etc., many of whom control America's institutions."[60] It is the domain of experts, or self-proclaimed experts, think-tank employees and politicians, and self-promoting public intellectuals. These are not boat-rockers; they have no essential quarrel with the direction or even existence of the boat, only the relative ranks of its crew members.

Despite the protestations of neutrality by NPR's defenders, listeners thereto, in all political camps, detect ideological shading, at least judging from their news-source preferences. A year-long 2014 project of the Pew Research Center endeavored to find how liberals and conservatives obtained their information about government and politics. The sample consisted of 2901 adults in the Pew Center's American Trends Panel. Given the long-standing ideological coloration of most media sources, it was no surprise that "consistent conservatives" were "tightly clustered around a single news source," with 47% "citing Fox News as their main source for news about government and politics." They were more distrustful than trustful of 24 of the 36 news sources.[61]

Liberals, by contrast, trusted more than distrusted 28 of those sources, with the single most trusted source among liberals—more than the *New York Times*, the *Washington Post*, ABC News, NBC News, CBS News, CNN, and even the BBC—being NPR. Fully 72% of liberals polled trusted NPR, with 9% registering distrust.[62] This state of affairs can be attributed to confirmation bias, given the political leanings of

NPR, and to the seeming trustworthiness of an institution that claims no profit motive, despite the fact that the same incentives are in play as those of profit-seeking broadcasters. (The eight sources liberals distrusted more than trusted were *The Blaze*, Fox News—tops at 81% distrust—Breitbart, Drudge Report, Sean Hannity Show, Glenn Beck Program, Rush Limbaugh Show, and Buzzfeed. The only source more distrusted than trusted by both liberals and conservatives was the clickbait site Buzzfeed.[63]) "Consistent liberals" relied on a wider pool of sources than did consistent conservatives, with CNN the most often cited (15%) and NPR a close second at 13%, followed by MSNBC (12%) and the *New York Times* (10%).[64]

NPR was singled out by Pew for the sharp ideological profile of its listeners. More "consistent liberals" (53%) reported having listened to NPR in the past week, even more than had watched CNN (52%), but that number plummets in the group marked "mostly liberal" to 23%. "[T]he public radio news network is far less central to the news diets of those in the other ideological groups," note the Pew authors.[65] It can be fairly characterized as the primary news source for consistent—some might say purist, others knee-jerk—liberals, and no one else.

But its profile remains lower silhouette than other news sources. Among those with "ideologically mixed political views," almost two-thirds—65%—had never even heard of NPR![66] This was a marginal improvement over a 1981 Roper Poll which found that fewer than one in four Americans (23%) had heard of National Public Radio.[67]

An Ingrown, Incestuous Culture

NPR's coverage of Barack Obama's inauguration gave brown-nosing sycophancy a bad name. Michel Martin, host of *Tell Me More*, fawned over that magical day when "people of all ages, people of every race and color, mostly smiling…were wishing each other well, like they do in those movies set on a mythic Christmas morning in a small town you didn't know existed. They were all heading off, in the same direction, with the determination of a mission, yet with a lightness of step. And they kept coming…and coming…and coming. Everywhere we looked, more people, more faces. Faces filled with cheer, with hope, and later, as the oath was taken, with tears."[68] The Korean Central News Agency, state press agency of Kim Jong-un's North Korea, couldn't have said it any better.

Contrast this tongue-bath with NPR's coverage of Donald Trump's inauguration eight years later. Typical was the Inauguration Day eve observation of political reporters Domenico Montanaro and Dana Farrington, who said that while "conservative America" was experiencing "jubilation": "There are hard feelings—and fear—in the other America. That America sees Trump's win as unfair and unjust—given Hillary Clinton won the popular vote by almost 3 million votes, given Russian meddling in the election intended to boost Trump, and given the unprecedented way Trump presented himself during the campaign. He went after all comers. No one was beyond reproach or the basest insult."[69]

Halfway into the Obama presidency, PBS supporters organized a "Million Puppet March" on Washington during the 2012 presidential election after Republican candidate Mitt Romney said during a debate that he would seek to terminate public broadcasting subsidies because "I'm not going to keep on spending money on things to borrow money from China to pay for."[70] (There may have been 1000 puppets and their puppeteers, not one million, though advanced math has never been a strong suit of marionettes.)

The moral preening of public broadcasting reached crisis levels in the Obama years. NPR CEO Vivian Schiller boasted that "NPR is no ordinary media company. No one talks about shareholder value. There are no daily Nielsen ratings being picked over to drive decisions for the next day."[71] Well of course not: rather than needing to satisfy individual consumers in the marketplace, NPR must satisfy, first and foremost, the government, and it does so quite successfully during Democratic administrations.

Ellen Weiss, senior vice president for news, proudly pointed to her organization's shift from real words to acronyms. "[W]e branded ourselves NPR and NPR NEWS instead of National Public Radio. We're not just national; we're international, and we have been for some time."[72] They had transcended the petty boundaries of the nation just in time for a worldwide revolt of populists and nationalists of both left and right against globalism.

The triumph of acronyms over words was made official in July 2010, when NPR headquarters in Washington DC ordered its staff and 900 or so affiliated stations to "use only the initials on the air or online."[73] The reason given by CEO Schiller was that "NPR is more modern, streamlined" than the erstwhile three-word title, which no one to that point in time had ever regarded as antiquated or a mouthful. She adduced CNN, the former Cable News Network, as an example, and it was a telling example, for CNN is about as unadventurous and un-offbeat a news-gathering organization as one can find. Schiller might as well have referenced KFC, née Kentucky Fried Chicken, as well: a mass-market purveyor of routine fare that changed its name in order to distance itself from its past and its associations, which in that case included the unfashionable state of Kentucky and the unfashionable form of food called fried. There was grumbling at public radio's grass roots, reported the *Washington Post*, but by 2010 the localism that was once promised to undergird National Public Radio had gone the way of storefront stations in the ghetto—it was no longer who or what NPR was.

Not long after, Weiss became a *former* senior vice president for news and Schiller became a *former* president and CEO when they resigned in separate incidents after seeming to play their parts perfectly—if, that is, they were starring in a show designed to confirm every conservative and right-wing suspicion of NPR's bias.[74] Weiss was the first to go, done in by her own intolerance of political diversity. The controversy involved NPR senior news analyst Juan Williams, a former *Washington Post* correspondent and author of the acclaimed history of the civil rights movement *Eyes on the Prize* (1987), among other books. Williams had long exhibited a heterodox streak, evidenced by his authorship of both a laudatory biography of U.S. Supreme Court Justice Thurgood Marshall (2000) and a sympathetic and incisive 1987 profile in the *Atlantic Monthly* of his friend Clarence Thomas, who would go on to serve as a Supreme Court justice who was, in the eyes of many, the antithesis of Justice Marshall. In other words, Williams was not easy to pigeonhole, and he had the virtues of writing well and speaking his mind without fear of reprimand. (In fact, Williams had published an op-ed in the *Post* during the Clarence Thomas hearings that defended the nominee—an act that his critics had not forgotten. Payback came a quarter-century later.)

Appearing in October 2010 on the Fox television show *The O'Reilly Factor*— itself virtually a fireable offense, given Fox's social and political remoteness from NPR and its audience—Williams was asked by host Bill O'Reilly to comment on the "Muslim dilemma," which O'Reilly framed in this way: "The cold truth is that in the world today jihad, aided and abetted by some Muslim nations, is the biggest threat on the planet." In the course of his response Williams spoke frankly: "I mean, look, Bill, I'm not a bigot. You know the kind of books I've written about the civil rights movement in this country. But when I get on the plane, I got to tell you, if I see people who are in Muslim garb and I think, you know, they are identifying themselves first and foremost as Muslims, I get worried. I get nervous." He went on to reference a Pakistani immigrant who had sought, unsuccessfully, to bomb Times Square: "He said the war with Muslims, America's war is just beginning, first drop of blood. I don't think there's any way to get away from these facts."

These were certainly defensible, understandable remarks, whether or not one agrees with the sentiment behind them. But NPR panicked. Williams was summarily fired, as public-relations shills offered in defense the exculpatory information that (1) he had been asked to stop identifying himself as a "senior correspondent for NPR" when appearing on *The O'Reilly Factor*; (2) he had once said on Fox that Michelle Obama, in giving what he regarded as a firebrand speech, had "this 'Stokely Carmichael in a designer dress' thing going"—a clear act of lèse-majesté, though the interdiction upon joking about a First Lady's fashion choices ended rather quickly when Melania Trump supplanted Michelle Obama; and (3) it had received a grand total of 378 emails from listeners who objected to Mr. Williams in 2008. (If only he had soothed their ears with the typical bromides of upper-middle-class liberalism!) At all events, Williams was fired, according to an NPR statement, because his remarks "were inconsistent with our editorial standards and practices, and undermined his credibility as a news analyst with NPR."[75]

NPR executives soon discovered that there is life, and opinion, outside the echo chamber. This caught Vivian Schiller, the NPR CEO and former senior vice president and general manager of NYTimes.com, off guard. Juan Williams and his colleagues, she said, had been warned over and again not to "express views" in other venues that "they would not air in their role as an NPR journalist." (She did not specify "timid, safe liberalism," though perhaps that was implicit in her formulation.) "This is not a First Amendment issue," she wanly insisted, which would certainly be the case if NPR had not been created by federal edict and financed with federal funds. Schiller made the by now rote argument that NPR was not really a public entity, as its budget received no money directly from the federal government, though this is, of course, disingenuous, since the CPB sends funds to member stations which then turn around and send a portion back to NPR as dues and programming fees.[76]

To take the flip side of Schiller's remark, there is no First Amendment issue involved in the *abolition* or *privatization* of public broadcasting. The First Amendment bars Congress from restricting speech but does not authorize government sponsorship of speech. David Boaz of the Cato Institute has written of "the separation of news and state," which he explains in this way: "We wouldn't want the federal government to publish a national newspaper. Why should we have a government television network and a government radio network? If anything should be kept separate from government and politics, it's the news and public affairs programming that Americans watch. When the government brings us the news—with all the inevitable bias and spin—the government is putting its thumb on the scales of democracy. It's time for that to stop."[77] It was too late for Juan Williams to benefit from the removal of the government's thumb. The NPR board stood with Schiller and Weiss, at least in the first rush of criticism. Vice chairman of the board Dave Edwards of Milwaukee's WUWM claimed that "every board member I spoke to today is supportive of Vivian and the decision that was made by the management team"—the sort of good soldier/obedient bureaucrat answer that would have driven Bill Siemering nuts and confirmed Lewis Hill's anarchism.[78]

Schiller misstepped with her crack that Williams would be advised to keep his opinions of Muslims between himself and "his psychiatrist or his publicist," a line that James Hohmann of *Politico* said, "fed into the narrative that NPR is liberal, smug, and condescending." Jesse Jackson, among others, stood up for Williams. "NPR was wrong because they did not afford him freedom of speech. They did it in a way that was unfair. The context was he was arguing with Bill O'Reilly, saying why he should not be so virulently anti-Muslim," explained Reverend Jackson. "They've martyred him, taking him to another level both with his resources and his authority as a journalist." Jackson continued: "I think that some of this predisposition towards Fox was the reason for the 'gotcha.' If they did not want his point of view, they should have said, 'When your contract is over, you do not fit into our scheme of things. And then [Juan would] go gracefully and with dignity. But to fire him in that way, and then to suggest he should see a psychiatrist, it was beneath the character and reputation of NPR."

Coincidentally, Rev. Jackson was used as a counterexample in the Williams case by a right-wing congressman, Steve King (R-IA), who said, "NPR fired Juan Williams for expressing something that is a visceral fear that most everyone feels when they get on an airplane. However, Jesse Jackson remains in NPR's good graces despite once saying, 'there is nothing more painful to me at this stage in my life than to walk down the street and hear footsteps and start thinking about robbery—then look around and see somebody white and feel relieved.'"[79] Going a step, or an entire mile, further, Fox News chair Roger Ailes compared NPR's panjandrums to "Nazis."[80]

More temperately, if fired by a more authentic passion, the First Amendment-friendly journalist Nat Hentoff, a staunch supporter of NPR, ridiculed Schiller for namby-pambyism, in particular, her professed horror that Williams had "offended many" by his comments. "Oh my goodness, he offended listeners!" wrote Hentoff.

"NPR's CEO is committing her partially publicly funded network to political correctness! If I were on the NPR staff, I might now be picketing the building."[81] Predictably, there were no intrepid Hentoffs of NPR picketing the building.

NPR rode out the criticism for a couple of months, after which an internal investigation led to the (genteel) rolling of heads. The aforementioned Dave Edwards of WUWM, who had proclaimed board unanimity in support of Vivian Schiller, did something of a modified *volte-face* after the board, with the assistance of the law firm of Weil, Gotshal & Manges, conducted its post-mortem. In best bureaucratic fashion, the investigation protected the institution while leaving its employees vulnerable. It found Juan Williams's firing to be justified under the terms of his contract and "not caused by pressure from outside donors or pressure groups." But Ellen Weiss, the senior vice president whose hand had wielded the axe against Williams, resigned after the completion of the investigation, and CEO Vivian Schiller was "denied her 2010 bonus" due to her role in the affair. Dave Edwards disclaimed responsibility for forcing the resignation of Weiss, saying that it was Schiller's doing, while Schiller refused comment. It was not a case study in transparency. Edwards, rather like the owner of a tanking NFL team, professed confidence in Schiller's leadership, praising her for taking "responsibility," though just what it was she took responsibility for was not made clear, since the board would not admit that the firing of Williams was an offense against him or the principle of the free exchange of ideas. The focus, instead, was on the harmful publicity generated by the story, and the potential use of this incident by Republican critics of NPR.

For his part, Juan Williams characterized Weiss as "the keeper of a flame of liberal orthodoxy," saying, "I think she represented a very ingrown, incestuous culture in that institution that's not open to not only [*sic*] different ways of thinking but angry at the fact that I would even talk or be on Fox."[82] Two months later it was Vivian Schiller's turn in the stocks, and she was escorted thereto by a man sharing her surname but unrelated to her. This time, NPR was done in by a "video sting" orchestrated by James O'Keefe, whose Project Veritas specializes in undercover operations designed to expose political bias in ostensibly nonpartisan public, quasi-public, and private entities in order to, it proclaims, "achieve a more ethical and transparent society."[83] In this instance, two Project Veritas representatives set up a lunch date with a pair of NPR executives at Cafe Milano in Georgetown, a fashionable Italian-themed restaurant which advertises itself as a "power center for diplomats, politicians, journalists, broadcasters, lobbyists, entertainers," and, one supposes, any non-powerful peon who can afford the overpriced food.[84]

The Project Veritas reps, Shaughn Adeleye and Simon Templar (the latter a pseudonymic nod to the fictional character known as "The Saint"), impersonated wealthy Muslims with admitted ties to the radical Muslim Brotherhood. They were there, on behalf of the fictive Muslim Education Action Center Trust, to offer NPR senior vice president for development Ron Schiller (no relation to Vivian) and senior director of institutional giving Betsy Liley a possible gift of $5 million so that the views of Muslims might be more fully aired. No agreement was reached over the imaginary $5 million gift, but it turned out to be an awfully expensive lunch, at least reputation-wise, for Ron Schiller. For the chat over breadsticks at Cafe Milano was taped, and Schiller, unaware that his words would be heard by any other than a fellow NPR executive and two fake Muslims, unloaded on Republicans: "The current Republican Party, particularly the Tea Party, is fanatically involved in people's personal lives and very fundamental Christian—and I wouldn't even call it Christian. It's this weird evangelical kind of move… it's been hijacked by this group and that…".

One fake Muslim interjects, "The radical, racist, Islamophobic, Tea Party people?" to which Schiller responds: "It's not just Islamophobic, but really xenophobic. Basically, they believe in white, Middle America, gun-toting—it's pretty scary. They're seriously racist, racist people."

Schiller goes on to tout the virtues of Madeira wine, perhaps not the wisest conversational gambit with religiously orthodox Muslims. He might have wished that the discussion had remained centered on his oenophilia. But it did not. When asked about the Juan Williams firing, Schiller offered: "What NPR did I'm very proud of. What NPR stood for is a non-racist, non-bigoted, straightforward telling of the news. Our feeling is that if a person expresses his or her personal opinion, which anyone is entitled to do in a free society, they are compromised as a journalist. They can no longer fairly report. And the question we asked internally was, 'Can Juan Williams, when he makes a statement like that, can he report to the Muslim population, and be believed, for example?' He lost all credibility and that breaks your ethics as a journalist."

Schiller's most irritating, if not damaging, remarks, in eyes of his colleagues, was his contention that NPR ought to be weaned from federal funding: "Republicans play off the belief among the general population that most of our funding comes from the government. Very little of our funding comes from the government, but they act as if all our funding comes from the government… it is very clear that in the long run, we would be better off without federal funding. And the challenge right now is that if we lost it altogether, we'd have a lot of stations go dark."[85]

NPR went into damage control. Dana Davis Rehm, senior vice president of Marketing, Communications, and External Relations, offered a half-counterattack, half-apology: "The fraudulent organization represented in this video repeatedly pressed us to accept a $5 million check, with no strings attached, which we repeatedly refused to accept. We are appalled by the comments made by Ron Schiller in the video, which are contrary to what NPR stands for. Mr. Schiller announced last week that he is leaving NPR for another job."[86] Straining the limits of credulity, especially to later Trump-era readers, Rehm added, "NPR is fair and open-minded about the people we cover. Our reporting reflects those values every single day—in the civility of the programming, the range of opinions we reflect, and the diversity of the stories we tell."[87]

CEO Vivian Schiller offered no support to her co-surnamed colleague. "I consider them an affront to NPR as a news organization; those comments were really contrary to what we stand for, everything we do," she explained to the *New York Times*. She also decried his potentially harmful assertion that NPR would be better off without a place at the federal trough, saying of Ron Schiller's observations to that effect: "They have no basis in fact. Eliminating federal funding would profoundly damage public broadcasting as a whole. It is impossible to separate NPR and the stations; we are one and the same." (So much for the vaunted localism of Siemering and the founders!) Ron Schiller said he was sorry: "While the meeting I participated in turned out to be a ruse, I made statements during the course of the meeting that are counter to NPR's values and also not reflective of my own beliefs. I offer my sincere apology to those I offended."[88] The immediate upshot of the affair was that the Cafe Milano had one less bigshot at its tables.

Ron Schiller resigned to take a position at the Aspen Institute as director of the Harman-Eisner Artist-in-Residence program effective the next month, April 2011. The move had obviously been in the works well before the brouhaha. But hours after the storm broke, and Schiller made his resignation from NPR effective immediately, the Aspen Institute issued this statement: "Ron Schiller has informed us that, in light of the controversy surrounding his recent statements, he does not feel that it's in the best interests of the Aspen Institute for him to come work here." It was, as David Weigel noted in *Slate*, a "complete career tailspin."[89] Ron carried Vivian "not related" Schiller with him into the tailspin. For the day after the story broke, and Ron hastened his resignation, the NPR board accepted Vivian's resignation "with understanding, genuine regret, and great respect for her leadership of NPR these past two years," as the official statement by Dave Edwards read.

In a way, this was payback for Schiller's treatment of Juan Williams half a year earlier. James O'Keefe explained the sting's Middle Eastern theme: "My colleague Shaughn Adeleye, who posed as one of the members of the Muslim Brotherhood, was pretty offended with what happened with Juan Williams and he suggested looking into NPR after that incident back in the fall. My other colleague, Simon Templar, came up with the idea to have a Muslim angle since Juan Williams was fired due to his comments. So we decided to see if there was a greater truth or hidden truth amongst these reporters and journalists and executives."[90]

The most active House advocate of defunding NPR, Rep. Doug Lamborn (R-CO), made swift use of Ron Schiller's lunch-time confession: "The fact that [Schiller threw] the racism around cavalierly is bothering to me," he told the *Atlantic*, "but the biggest admission that I picked up on is that they could survive and actually be better off without federal funding, and actually that is true for a lot of reasons. They'd have more independence. Congress wouldn't be breathing down their necks, and they do have some quality products that the private market, the free market would be very eager to support. It's not an essential government function," Rep. Lamborn continued. "Maybe at one point 40 years ago when all you had were three major networks, and that was pretty much it, you could make a smart-bidder argument, but today there are so many media outlets available in so many formats that people thought inconceivable just a few years ago... it's outlived the reason it was originally created."[91]

But it kept on living. Barbs from the right and brickbats from the left bounced off NPR like rubber arrows from a child's bow. An attempt by Republicans to defund NPR in the immediate aftermath of the O'Keefe tape passed the House by a largely party-line vote of 228–192 but made no headway in the Senate.[92] The method of defunding proposed was to bar stations from using federal monies to purchase NPR programming, which would have kept the spigot turned on but redirected its ulti-mate beneficiary from NPR's Washington headquarters to other, presumably more decentralized, producers. Perhaps the most amusing defense of NPR during this flurry of activity came from Rep. Earl Blumenauer, an Oregon Democrat, who said, presumably straight-faced, "National Public Radio is one of the few areas where the American public can actually get balanced information."[93]

Rep. Lamborn has remained a thorn in public radio's side, reintroducing his bill to prohibit federal funding of National Public Radio, though without chance of success in the currently Democratic-controlled Congress.

While NPR tends not to flatter capitalists and businesspeople in its coverage—unless they are "woke" Silicon Valley types or feminists who write books about breaking glass ceilings—its own internal labor practices would put a caricatured 19th-century robber baron to shame. As the *Washington Post* reported—perhaps somewhat gleefully, given that the *Post* and Washington's leading NPR station, WAMU, are media competitors—public radio in our nation's capital is heavily reliant on tempo-rary employees, or "temps," usually young employees who come and go, depending on the whims and needs of the employer, and who "do almost every important job in NPR's newsroom," from pitching stories to booking guests and writing interview questions and editing.

Most news organizations utilize temps, though in nowhere near the numbers that government-subsidized NPR does. According to the Radio Television Digital News Association, the average radio station has just one temp or part-timer on staff. At NPR's Washington newsroom, which sends out to the world *All Things Considered* and *Morning Edition*, upwards of 20% of the "union-covered newsroom workforce" of 483 people are temp workers.

Temps interviewed by the *Washington Post* repeatedly described their relation-ship with NPR as "exploitative." They had the usual complaints of any employee—management doesn't communicate well enough, they are underappreciated, etc.—but in addition, their employment is "stressful" and "precarious," often for just a week or a fortnight, depending upon the news cycle, the vacations and sick leaves of regular employees, and other variables. They are covered and then uncovered by health insur-ance; they are drawing a paycheck one week and sitting home waiting for the phone to ring the next.

What makes this different from the typical experience of temporary employees is that NPR's temps labor for a news source whose editorial bias is squarely within the liberal Democratic camp. NPR has run frequent stories about debates in Wash-ington and around the country over increasing the minimum wage and increasing government subsidies or guarantees to the uninsured, and yet the organization's own labor practices contradict its ingrained editorial bias. In fact, the *Post* reported that during negotiations over the most recent three-year labor contract, NPR manage-ment "proposed eliminating all benefits for temps (except those required by law), including health insurance and holiday pay."[94] They talk the talk—incessantly, and in those curiously de-sexed and placeless accents of the archetypal NPR announcer—but rather than walking the walk they tell their lowest-paid and most vulnerable employees to take a hike.

That's not the only newsroom scandal in the Washington office. In 2017, Michael Oreskes, the former *New York Times* Washington bureau chief who in 2015 had been named NPR's senior vice president of news and editorial director, was hit with a flurry of charges that he had harassed women sexually while at the *New York Times* and behaved in a gross manner during his two years in the radio newsroom, without consequence. The first complaint was lodged by 26-year-old assistant producer Rebecca Hersher, who said that Oreskes, several months after joining NPR, had launched into a discourse about his "sex girlfriend" during a business conversation. Hersher reported the conversation to management, which gave Oreskes the wrist-slap known as a "warning." NPR CEO Jarl Mohn told the *Washington Post* that "We put him on notice that this could not occur" again. The punishment sounded about as harsh as *Animal House*'s double secret probation.

In the following year, two women reported that while at the *Times*, Oreskes had kissed them, forcing his tongue into their mouths, in separate instances. And despite Mohn's limp admonition, Oreskes allegedly continued this behavior, which the *Post* reported as ranging from "inappropriate conversations with young female employees to what one described as 'spontaneous kissing.'" (The latter is a perhaps unfortunate locution, as its opposite, premeditated kissing, is a rarer thing.)

Oreskes's behavior was "an open secret in the newsroom," and his improprieties, combined with the organization's feeble response, "stirred a virtual rebellion… particularly among female employees." They expressed their displeasure via petition, and NPR, media spotlight suddenly shining upon its internal discontent, fired Oreskes on Halloween 2017.[95] The black eye for NPR soon faded. The #MeToo movement did not demand a reduction in the CPB budget. As for Oreskes, in late 2018 he teamed with two former Fox News executives to create La Corte News, an aggregated news site.[96]

And NPR rattled on.

Notes of Chapter

1. Kim McAvoy, "Public broadcasters go on offense," *Broadcasting & Cable* (December 19, 1994): 48. NPR's national board of directors currently consists of 23 members, of which a majority—12—are station managers elected by their peers, nine are "prominent members of the public" elected by the rest of the board, and the others are the foundation chair president and CEO. Although it is a federally begotten entity, its board is chosen neither by the executive nor the legislative branch of the federal government. "NPR Board Welcomes New Public Director," NPR, March 13, 2019, www.npr.org.

2. Karen De Witt, "Gingrich Foresees a World Without Public Broadcasting," *New York Times*, December 16, 1994.

3. Patricia M. Chuh, "The Fate of Public Broadcasting in the Face of Federal Funding Cuts," *Commlaw Conspectus*, Vol. 3, No. 2 (Summer 1995): 218.

4. *This is NPR: The First Forty Years*, p. 166.

5. McAvoy, "Public broadcasters go on offense," *Broadcasting & Cable*.

6. Elizabeth Rathburn, "Congress keeps up threat to public broadcasting," *Broadcasting & Cable* (January 23, 1995): 10.

7. De Witt, "Gingrich Foresees a World Without Public Broadcasting," *New York Times*.

8. Chuh, "The Fate of Public Broadcasting in the Face of Federal Funding Cuts," *Commlaw Conspectus*: 216.

9. Ibid.: 215.

10. Ellen Edwards, "The $92,000 Questions," *Washington Post*, February 14, 1995.

11. George Archibald, "Public broadcasting's federal subsidy far exceeds appropriation," *Washington Times*, February 19, 1995.

12. McAvoy, "Public broadcasters go on offense," *Broadcasting & Cable*.

13. Rathburn, "Congress keeps up threat to public broadcasting," *Broadcasting & Cable*: 10.

14. Elizabeth Rathbun, "Public broadcasters look elsewhere for funds," *Broadcasting & Cable*, February 27, 1995, p. 18.

15. De Witt, "Gingrich Foresees a World Without Public Broadcasting," *New York Times*.

16. Judy Mann, "Keeping a Hand in Public Broadcasting," *Washington Post*, February 24, 1995.

17. William G. Mayer, "Why talk radio is conservative," *Public Interest* (Summer 2004).

18. Montopoli, "All Things Considerate," *Washington Monthly*.

19. Mayer, "Why talk radio is conservative," *Public Interest*.

20. Paul Farhi, "Big Bird Taken Off Death Row," *Washington Post*, July 13, 1995.

21. Chuh, "The Fate of Public Broadcasting in the Face of Federal Funding Cuts," *Commlaw Conspectus*: 213.

22. Farhi, "Big Bird Taken Off Death Row," *Washington Post*.

23. Mitchell, *Listener Supported: The Culture and History of Public Radio*, p. 166.

24. Walker, *Rebels on the Air: An Alternative History of Radio in America*, p. 301.

25. *This is NPR: The First Forty Years*, p. 166.

26. Barlow, "Community radio in the US: the struggle for a democratic medium," *Media, Culture and Society*: 89.

27. Looker, *The Sound and the Story: NPR and the Art of Radio*, p. 115.

28. Barlow, "Community radio in the US: the struggle for a democratic medium," *Media, Culture and Society*: 83.

29. "Statement of Victor Gold, April 6, 1993," in *Public Broadcasting and the Public Trust*, p. 229.

30. Ibid., pp. 230–231.

31. "History," https://kpfa.org/about/history/, accessed May 27, 2019.

32. Looker, *The Sound and the Story: NPR and the Art of Radio*, p. 115.

33. Walker, *Rebels on the Air: An Alternative History of Radio in America*, pp. 135–136.

34. Boaz, "Ending Taxpayer Funding for Public Broadcasting."

35. David Boaz, "Defund PBS," *Baltimore Sun*, June 27, 2005.

36. Husseini, "The Broken Promise of Public Radio," *The Humanist*: 26.

37. Fox, "NPR Grows Up," *American Journalism Review*.

38.   Howard Husock, "Public broadcasting shouldn't get a handout from taxpayers anymore," *Washington Post*, March 17, 2017.
39.   *This is NPR: The First Forty Years*, p. 225.
40.   "'Ray and Joan' Chronicles Complex Life Of Kroc's Philanthropic Wife," November 19, 2016, https://www.npr.org/2016/11/19/502685423/-ray-and-joan-chronicles-complicated-life-of-a-philanthropist-who-gave-away-mcdo.
41.   Husock, "Public broadcasting shouldn't get a handout from taxpayers anymore," *Washington Post*.
42.   Sheldon L. Richman, Testimony before the Subcommittee on Energy and Mineral Resources of the U.S. House of Representatives, January 19, 1995.
43.   Mitchell, *Listener Supported: The Culture and History of Public Radio*, p. 145.
44.   Trevor Burrus, "Public Broadcasting: The Problem is Tilt, Not Bias," *Daily Caller*, www.dailycaller.com, March 21, 2011.
45.   Kosof, "Public Radio—Americans Want More," in *Radio: The Forgotten Medium*, p. 175.
46.   Lisa de Moraes, "PBS Chief Paula Kerger Responds to Third Donald Trump Push to De-Fund," Deadline.com, March 18, 2019.
47.   Arnold Steinberg, "Public Television and Radio Remain Unconstitutional," *The American Spectator*, March 24, 2017, www.spectator.org.
48.   Richman, Testimony before the Subcommittee on Energy and Mineral Resources of the U.S. House of Representatives.
49.   David Boaz, "Scandal in Public Broadcasting," *Cato at Liberty*, August 30, 2006, www.cato.org.
50.   David Boaz, "Top Ten Reasons to Privatize Public Broadcasting," FoxNews.com, July 25, 2005.
51.   Clark, "Public Broadcasting," *CQ Researcher*: 6, 9, 10.
52.   Montopoli, "All Things Considerate," *Washington Monthly*.
53.   Derek Hunter, *Outrage, Inc.: How the Liberal Mob Ruined Science, Journalism, and Hollywood* (New York: HarperCollins, 2018), pp. 143–44.
54.   David Boaz, "Is Public Broadcasting Biased?" http://blogs.brittanica.com, April 4, 2011.
55.   Ryan Bourne, "It's Time for Broadcasters to Start Confronting Their Anti-Right Bias," www.cityam.com, January 30, 2018.
56.   Robert M. Eisinger, Loring R. Veenstra, and John P. Koehn, "What Media Bias? Conservative and Liberal Labeling in Major U.S. Newspapers," *Press/Politics* 12, No. 1 (Winter 2007): 21.
57.   Boaz, "Defund PBS," *Baltimore Sun*.
58.   Mitchell, *Listener Supported: The Culture and History of Public Radio*, p. 179.
59.   Huber, "The Static at National Public Radio," Heritage Foundation. See also "NPR programming attacked by conservatives," *Broadcasting*, June 24, 1985.
60.   Gonzalez, "Is There Any Justification for Continuing to Ask Taxpayers to Fund NPR and PBS?" Knight Foundation.
61.   "Political Polarization & Media Habits: From Fox News to Facebook, How Liberals and Conservatives Keep Up with Politics," Pew Research Center, October 2014, p. 2.

62. Ibid., p. 49.
63. Ibid., p. 5.
64. Ibid., pp. 4, 11.
65. Ibid., p. 21.
66. Ibid., p. 51.
67. Kinsley, "None Dare Call it Commercial," *Harper's*: 12.
68. *This is NPR: The First Forty Years*, p. 256.
69. Domenico Montanaro and Dan Farrington, "What To Expect For Donald Trump's Inauguration," NPR, January 19, 2017, https://www.npr.org/2017/01/19/510664274/what-to-expect-for-donald-trumps-inauguration.
70. Trevor Burrus, "Big Bird's Fuzzy Defenders March on Washington," *USA Today*, October 31, 2012.
71. *This is NPR: The First Forty Years*, p. 259.
72. Ibid., p. 267.
73. Paul Farhi, "National Public Radio is changing its name to NPR," *Washington Post*, May 28, 2019.
74. Elizabeth Jensen, "NPR's Costly Mistake," January 7, 2011, https://www.npr.org/sections/publiceditor/2011/01/07/132718863/nprs-costly-mistake.
75. Brian Stelter, "NPR Fires Analyst Over Comments on Muslims," *New York Times*, October 21, 2010; Brian Stelter and Elizabeth Jensen, "NPR Defends Firing Williams as Criticism Mounts," *New York Times*, October 22, 2010.
76. Stelter and Jensen, "NPR Defends Firing Williams as Criticism Mounts," *New York Times*.
77. David Boaz, "Privatizing Public Broadcasting," www.cato.org, March 3, 2011.
78. Stelter and Jensen, "NPR Defends Firing Williams as Criticism Mounts," *New York Times*.
79. James Hohmann, "Jesse Jackson condemns Williams firing," www.politico.com, October 27, 2010.
80. Elizabeth Jensen, "NPR Executive Who Fired Juan Williams Resigns," *New York Times*, January 6, 2011.
81. Nat Hentoff, "NPR Was Wrong—But Don't Cut Their Funding," www.cato.org, October 27, 2010.
82. Jensen, "NPR Executive Who Fired Juan Williams Resigns," *New York Times*.
83. "About Project Veritas," www.projectveritas.com, accessed August 1, 2019.
84. "About," www.cafemilano.com, accessed August 1, 2019.
85. David Weigel, "James O'Keefe Versus NPR," www.slate.com, March 8, 2011.
86. Keach Hagey, "NPR exec: tea party is 'scary, racist,'" *Politico*, www.politico.com, March 8, 2011.
87. "NPR CEO Vivian Schiller resigns," CNN Wire Staff, www.cnn.com, March 10, 2011.
88. Brian Stelter and Elizabeth Jensen, "Facing Lawmakers' Fire, NPR Sees New Setback," *New York Times*, March 9, 2011.
89. David Weigel, "Ron Schiller Won't Join Aspen Institute After All," www.slate.com, March 9, 2011.
90. "NPR CEO Vivian Schiller resigns," CNN Wire Staff, www.cnn.com.

91. Chris Good, "What James O'Keefe's Latest Video Means for NPR Funding," www.theatlantic.com, March 8, 2011.

92. "House votes to stop NPR funding," www.cnn.com, March 17, 2011. See also Nat Hentoff, "Republicans' Assault on NPR and PBS," www.cato.org, March 30, 2011.

93. Glenn J. McLoughlin and Lena A. Gomez, "The Corporation for Public Broadcasting: Federal Funding and Issues," Congressional Research Service, May 3, 2017, p. 6.

94. Paul Farhi, "At NPR, an army of temps face uphill battle," *Washington Post*, December 10, 2018.

95. Paul Farhi, "NPR bosses knew about harassment allegations, but kept top editor on job," *Washington Post*, November 1, 2017.

96. Jason Schwartz, "Ousted NPR news chief, ex-Fox News execs team up on new site," www.politico.com, December 18, 2018.

Chapter 8
Conclusion: What Is to Be Done?

Donald Trump, too, sought to terminate funding for the Corporation for Public Broadcasting. He made even less headway in this attempt than did his Republican predecessors, though the effort, or at least the effort of Office of Management and Budget director Mick Mulvaney, did win praise from one of Trump's harshest critics, George Will, who noted wryly that in the event NPR disappeared, "Listeners to public radio might have to make do with America's 4666 AM and 6754 FM commercial stations, 437 satellite radio channels, perhaps 70,000 [*sic*] (the number is likely ten times that) podcasts, and other Internet and streaming services."[1] As Will notes, public broadcasting has achieved a kind of bureaucratic immortality, perhaps tied to its upper-middle-class constituency, which does not lack articulate and insistent voices.

CPB harrumphed loudly at this act of lèse-majesté by President Trump, issuing a statement asserting that the "elimination of federal funding to CPB would initially devastate and ultimately destroy public media's role in early childhood education, public safety, connecting citizens to our history, and promoting civil discussions—all for Americans in both rural and urban communities."[2] That post-dash clause was a nod to the red staters and acknowledgement of new, or at least temporary, political realities. Yet critics persist. Especially constructive critics. After all, grousing is no program. Although it sometimes seems as if conservative disparagers of NPR would flip to being supporters if only it sounded like a Fox News of the radio, more principled critics have proposed various reforms, up to and including abolition.

The oft-repeated claim by funding advocates that public television recipients, on average, derive just 15% of their revenue from the CPB and NPR stations derive a much smaller share suggests that most stations could adapt quite easily to the withdrawal of federal monies on a phase-out schedule of perhaps five years. (These claims are disingenuous, as NPR defenders often omit the community service grants—that is, money the CPB sends to local stations, which then use it to buy programming from NPR—from their calculations. If one adds in state and local government contributions, taxpayer funding makes up slightly over one-third of the revenue of PBS stations and perhaps 15–20% of the revenue of the average NPR station.[3]) In any event, such a phase-out plan remains outside mainstream discussion, although the right wing of House Republicans nurture it still. But there are sporadic signs that those outside the political Right are also thinking about the airwaves without NPR, or at least with a much different NPR.

For the universe of audio offerings has exploded in recent years, to the point that many consider public radio superfluous. Eric Nuzum, an NPR vice president for programming who left for the commercial market in 2015, remarks, "Part of the public radio value equation has been that it was a very unique island in a sea of mediocrity and other audio entertainment." Due to podcasting and similar programming, "That is no longer the case."[4] There are an estimated 700,000 podcasts on the market today covering a dizzying array of subjects that range from Indian cooking to planetary astronomy, from politics to punk rock, from religious iconography to the history of New Orleans.[5] Podcasters not only enjoy a freedom of outlook and subject not shared by NPR reporters, but they also enter a field without the enormous obstacles faced by would-be broadcasters: they don't need a license, and they don't have to build a tower.

Jim Epstein, who worked from 2002 to 2009 as a producer at WNET in New York, has argued that government funding of public media is not only unnecessary but also actually harmful. In the case of NPR, while it produces popular and quality podcasts, organizational policy prohibits "hosts from promoting podcasts on the radio or from even mentioning NPR's popular smartphone app." Nor are episodes of *Morning Edition* and *All Things Considered* available in podcast format. And as Adam Davidson, an NPR reporter who departed for the podcasting world, has observed, podcasters "have a creative freedom that NPR's institutional frictions simply can't allow."[6]

David Boaz notes, "PBS used to ask: 'If not PBS, then who?' The answer now is: HBO, Bravo, Discovery, History, History International, Science, Planet Green, Sundance, Military, C-SPAN 1/2/3" and several hundreds more.[7] In George Will's phrase, the argument that public television filled a void in the vast wasteland had been "obviated by technology."[8] The situation in radio is not exactly analogous, but the profusion of alternative channels is just as overwhelming with, for instance, Sirius Radio, whose satellite and online radio services have greatly expanded the universe of literate and listenable, not to mention bizarre, choices. Sirius alone offers such channels as E Street Radio, The Catholic Channel, Canadian Indigenous Peoples' Radio, Krishna Das Yoga Radio—a head-spinning variety that makes NPR look monochromatic and monovocal.

To regain relevance, Jim Epstein, the former WNET producer, proposes that NPR (and PBS) "privatize and charge a monthly subscription fee." Alternatively, their revenue from individuals, foundations, and businesses, which currently comprises about 60% of public radio's funding, would be more than sufficient to distribute their content free of charge, as is now the case, if they rid themselves of the "massive overhead costs" associated with the 1400 or so NPR and PBS stations.[9]

In 2017, to mark the 50th anniversary of the Public Broadcasting Act, the John S. and James L. Knight Foundation commissioned six separate reports assessing the current need for a public (that is, taxpayer-funded) media and, if so, how it might be modified or remade to meet changing realities.[10] Knight asked "thinkers across the spectrum"—including, to its credit, skeptics of the value or contemporary relevance of public broadcasting—to address a pair of questions:

1. Do we still need a public media? If so, why?
2. How should public media be destroyed, disrupted or restructured to inform community today?[11]

Suggestions with respect to NPR were diverse and sometimes interesting. Melody Kramer and Betsy O'Donovan, a former digital strategist for NPR and the executive director of the University of North Carolina's *Daily Tar Heel*, respectively, urged that public media refocus on "programming for children," going so far as to say "That's what public media should be and do. Only that. Seriously." Specifically, "children from America's poor, immigrant or minority communities" should be served, which leaves a large segment of the youth population unserved, including the working-class whites whose communities have been devastated by the opioid epidemic and the hollowing out of the Rust Belt and the industrial sector. But a lot of their parents probably voted for Trump, so they may be, in the eyes of the public broadcasting establishment, irredeemable if not thoroughly deplorable.

The "basic mission of public media," writes Kramer and O'Donovan, is encased in the question, "What *kind* of citizen are we creating?"[12] This is a basic question of any community, any society, although the introduction of government, with its unique powers of coercion, complicates matters. Not to overstate things, but molding citizens to the state's desires was the goal of Soviet and Nazi media. If government-subsidized media are granted the means to create certain kinds of citizens, won't those be the kind of citizens who are most useful to the powers-that-be? Won't the values and beliefs inculcated by the public media be those values and beliefs that best serve the state? Kramer and O'Donovan acknowledge the danger of a *Pravda*-like public media which acts as a mouthpiece of and ideological enforcer for an all-powerful (or yearning to be all-powerful) government, but granting *any* media outlet the resources and the license to mold citizens is a step down a road that leads to a future of bleak conformity, mass servility, and cookie-cutterism rampant.

Sue Gardner, a former executive with Wikimedia and the Canadian Broadcasting Company, began her paper with an epigram that effectively conveyed the tone of her work: "I like to pay my taxes; with them I buy civilization." Gardner admires the British Broadcasting Corporation, which was founded in 1922 by the nation's top manufacturers of radios but nationalized in 1927 as a public corporation. As Gardner quotes the responsible parliamentary committee's 1926 report, radio broadcasting "carries with it such great propaganda power that it cannot be trusted to any person or bodies other than a public corporation." So to avoid the danger of propaganda, the government was given charge of the nascent industry!

Gardner emphasizes the BBC's role as builder of "social cohesion" and an informational link between state and citizen. A cynic might rephrase this to say that government radio works to ensure greater uniformity of opinion, with the acceptable opinion being that of the political, financial, and social establishment. Though acknowledging the profusion of alternatives to commercial radio today, she urges a renewed emphasis on public broadcasting in order to "heal the rift between the people and the institutions intended to serve them." She is troubled by the election of Donald Trump and the rise of anti-establishment parties around the world; "in liberal democracies," she laments, "large numbers of people believe political elites are no longer representing their interests." The antidote, it seems, is a big dose of government-subsidized radio and television to convince them otherwise.

In a passage that might have been written as a parody by some conspiracy-monger convinced that the elites are trying to control the thoughts of the rabble and mold their political views in conformance with the views of the elites, Gardner writes: "Research shows that people exposed to news on public television are better-informed than those exposed to news on private TV. They are likelier to vote, and have *more realistic perceptions* [emphasis added] of their societies, especially on issues related to crime and immigration. They are less likely to express negative attitudes toward immigrants. Countries with strong public broadcasters have higher levels of social trust, and the people who live in them are less likely to hold extremist political views."

The purpose of public broadcasting, in this formulation, is to bridge the gap between elite and popular opinion by convincing the plebs that the elites are right, and that they should alter their views in accordance with the elite-sponsored views propounded on public radio and television. We put aside the question of the content of those views, which Gardner contrasts as "realistic" (elite) and tending toward the "extremist" (popular).[13] Hers is a call for a renewed propaganda campaign waged, in effect, for the elites and against what they regard as their social, intellectual, financial, and moral inferiors. In our age of resurgent populism, it is unlikely to attract much support outside those powerful enough to directly benefit therefrom.

Apropos, the Cold War era radio outlets funded by the U.S. government to broadcast to those living under communism or other repressive systems—Voice of America and Radio Marti (Cuba)—had been, until 2013, barred from broadcasting to the domestic audience. As Senator Edward Zorinsky (D-NE) said in 1985, "The American taxpayer does not need or want his tax dollars used to support U.S. government propaganda directed at him or her."[14] The purpose of these so-called USIB (U.S. International Broadcasting) agencies, whose roots date back to the Second World War and the beginning of the Cold War, was to "create a better understanding of our nation with a foreign populace as a whole by providing them access to American culture, history, law, society, art, and music that might not be otherwise available through standard local media outlets."[15] Though the authors and executors of these agencies denied that they were engaging in propaganda, the fact that Americans were unable to listen in on what their national government was telling the world suggested that perhaps the information conveyed was not, strictly speaking, accurate. Certainly, the suspicion was that the VOA and Radio Marti lacked subtlety—but surely Sue Gardner's envisaged aural tool by which "extremists" can be converted to "realists" would be subtle in the, well, extreme.

More consistent with the dreams of the early advocates of educational broadcasting, and striking a more innovative and populist note, Adam Ragusea of Mercer University advocates a complete rebuilding of the public broadcasting model to a "widely-dispersed system of nonprofit, user-supported local news organizations specializing in public service journalism and publishing primarily online, primarily in text—in other words, a *ProPublica* (the liberal nonprofit investigative news service based in New York City) in every city, made economically feasible by government subsidies."

Ragusea notes the generally poor record of public radio and television in covering local news, culture, and events. Quoting a Knight report of September 2009 which concluded that "Public stations do not have a strong record of spearheading local investigative journalism, and most public radio broadcasters have little or no local news reporting staff," he advocates a new dedication to local reporting, which of course was contemplated by the localist faction during the debates of the 1960s.[16] (NPR would respond that 90% of member stations today offer local news during weekday drive times, though this is not infrequently a rehash of whatever appears in the local morning newspaper.[17])

The decline of local newspapers—newspaper newsroom employment fell by 47% (71,000 to 38,000) between 2008 and 2018—has eroded or even eliminated the only source of reportage on community affairs in many cities.[18] Curiously, journalistic employment has remained fairly constant in New York City and has even grown in Washington DC, and Los Angeles, due to digital outlets, but in smaller and mid-sized cities the situation is far less rosy. As a result, city and town councils, county legislatures, local zoning boards, and other governmental bodies whose decisions directly affect the way we live go almost completely uncovered in many parts of the country.

Ragusea, pointing to the great expense of radio broadcasting—not in salaries but rather in studios, towers, buildings, control centers, administrators, and fundraisers—suggests that perhaps NPR ought to abandon broadcasting and concentrate its efforts in online local journalism, supported by members, philanthropy, merchandising, and maybe—though not necessarily—government. The sale of their broadcasting licenses, he says, could provide an enormous windfall for the transition to the much less expensive—but more relevant and in some cases desperately needed—local online news nonprofit. (Sale of their licenses to commercial interests—the means by which a windfall might be obtained—is currently forbidden and would require a regulatory reversal.) More realistically and in the shorter term, he says, stations could devote more time and effort to online local news reporting, instancing such efforts at Minnesota Public Radio, St. Louis Public Radio, and Colorado Public Radio.

Of course, the withdrawal of federal monies from public broadcasting would spur unprecedentedly large private, corporate, and foundational contributions to NPR and PBS. It would be like Ronald Reagan, Jesse Helms, Newt Gingrich, and Donald Trump all wrapped up into one super-sized scare package. The donations would pour in like a Niagara Falls-quality cataract. Legal analyst Trevor Burrus suggests that if public broadcasting truly desires independence from the long leash of Washington, they should do the following: "Announce that you will be giving up government funding in an effort to free yourself from political pressure, create a noncommercial, nonprofit media entity that runs entirely on donations, and then hold the biggest fundraiser you've ever had." "I will gladly write the first check," adds Burrus, who probably needn't worry about opening his checkbook any time soon.[19]

Writing in the Knight Foundation series, Mike Gonzalez of the Heritage Foundation admits that the withdrawal of federal money from NPR would probably put the system under the financial sponsorship of the likes of George Soros and other left-of-center philanthropists, to which he responds, "So what? Liberal and conservative views are already funded by the private sector, at MSNBC and Fox for example, where they compete in the marketplace of ideas. The goal here is not to suppress one side or the other but to remove the tyranny to which Jefferson referred" in his famous lines from the Virginia Statute for Religious Freedom.[20]

The board of directors of the Corporation for Public Broadcasting has never been a nest of ornery independents, or even moderately fractious overseers, but one bright and shining exception to this rule was Howard Husock, a former producer, director, and reporter at public station WGBH in Boston, and a vice president at the free-market Manhattan Institute who was named to the board in 2013 as one of President Obama's mandated Republican appointees.

Husock boldly established himself as a generator and promoter of innovative and unwelcome ideas on the board, a role he played until his departure in 2018. To eye-rolling annoyance by his standpat colleagues, he sketched a "post-subsidy" future for both PBS and NPR, although he noted that the envisioned post-subsidy combination of a "no-cost license" and maintenance of nonprofit status would amount to very substantial subsidy indeed. He is willing to grant continuing federal support of children's television programming, the one aspect of PBS which enjoys widespread public support, and of the operating expenses of rural NPR stations, which would admittedly struggle in the absence of alms.

Most irritating to NPR is Husock's suggestion that local stations keep the money they currently receive in the form of those community service grants which they then turn over to the Washington-based headquarters in return for their airing of national programs. (In 2014, for instance, public radio stations received $223 million in community service grants; more than 83% of this sum, or $186 million, was simply recycled to NPR and the biggest producing stations.[21]) Given that consumers in this age of smartphones and the Internet can access these programs directly, local stations ought to retain these grants in order to nurture local journalism and reportage on issues meaningful to those in their immediate listening and viewing area. The result, of course, would be the accelerated irrelevance of Washington DC, in the world of public broadcasting.[22] But unless local stations "find ways to use their funding to produce content which can't be found on smartphones and tablets," warns Husock, "they will have no reason to exist."[23]

Dismissing the honeyed fantasies purveyed by NPR's partisans, Husock noted that trust in public radio divides sharply and predictably along regional, political, and economic lines. One could almost hear the gnashing of teeth by other board members as Husock pointed out that only one of NPR's ten highest-rated stations was located in the South (and that in liberal Raleigh-Durham, North Carolina) and that listeners in all markets are substantially better-off economically than are non-listeners. The way to lessen this upper-middle-class Northeastern and coastal liberal bias is not by hiring conservatives or offering token right-of-center shows, but by promoting local journalism by local stations. He imagines NPR relying much more on its member stations, with "[s]tories told empathetically and contextually, drawing on local concerns." For instance, he writes, "Think of the out-of-work coal miner whose situation makes clear the tradeoffs involved with changing energy policy," or the "mega-church that mounts efforts to help promote marriage—and doesn't just oppose gay marriage."

A reliance upon "the lively localism that has always made America great" would close the gap between NPR and the people whose taxes help to pay its bills. Short of shutting off the spigot—which Husock supports—this tack seems to him the most satisfactory solution to the problem of liberal bias in public broadcasting.[24] These ideas are kindred to those of the aforementioned Adam Ragusea. Husock asks us to imagine a nationwide network of upwards of 1000 radio stations and 350 television stations which, instead of simply airing programs made in Washington for Washingtonians, paid attention to their own backyards. He concedes that the presence of government subsidy complicates matters and "could undermine the integrity and credibility of public broadcasting's journalistic efforts," especially in cases in which a local school district or state-sponsored university holds the broadcast license.[25] But such a shift in emphasis would at least curtail the Beltway-centric reportage of public radio and perhaps invigorate moribund or dormant traditions of local news reporting. What a refreshing change it would be, he suggests, to tune in one's putatively local NPR station and hear "voices not typically heard in the Acela corridor."[26] It would be a way of validating the fustian so often spun by media talking heads who speak of the necessity of a well-informed citizenry to meaningfully democratic governance.

In a farewell essay when leaving the board at the end of 2018, Husock urged CPB members to "resist cheerleading the system" and insist on discussing programming in open sessions, as is not currently the case. He also expressed disapproval of the hoary Republican strategy of trying to force right-of-center programming on PBS and NPR. Better, he says, to invite "outsiders of varying perspectives to offer a critique" of programming, pointing out bias and neglected points of view.[27]

The withdrawal of CPB funds would, in the short term, pose challenges for many smaller radio stations; those sympathetic to public and community radio but critical of federal subsidy usually urge a gradual decline in funding for these rather than a cold-turkey regimen. For instance, Jesse Walker writes that "transitional funds should be earmarked for the small, rural stations that need them most, as opposed to the enormous NPR and PBS operations that mostly serve well-to-do urban and suburban audiences."[28] Walker has proposed turning the CPB into an independent trust fund with a "decentralized, democratic structure," though he suspects that many smaller stations would still find themselves as third-class citizens in a system dominated by upper-middle-class and professional interests.[29] In which case they would break away, perhaps to coalesce with stations of similar size and outlook.

Under such scenarios as sketched by Husock and Walker, national public radio would be local rather than national, and private and/or nonprofit rather than public, but it would more effectively and honestly and even exuberantly fulfill the promise of radio foreseen not only by the founders of National Public Radio but also by the early visionaries who once imagined that radio could be a tool of education and uplift and enlightenment.

Perhaps, someday, it may yet be.

Notes of Chapter

1. George Will, "Public broadcasting's immortality defies reason," *Washington Post*, June 3, 2017. "PBS is superfluous, but strangely immortal," Penn Live, https://www.pennlive.com/opinion/2017/06/pbs_is_superfluous_but_str ange.html, June 5, 2017.
2. Howard Husock, "Public broadcasting shouldn't get a handout from taxpayers anymore," *Washington Post*, March 17, 2017.
3. Gonzalez, "Is There Any Justification for Continuing to Ask Taxpayers to Fund NPR and PBS?" Knight Foundation.
4. Adam Ragusea, "Topple the Towers: Why Public Radio and Television Stations Should Radically Reorient Toward Digital-First Local News, and How They Could Do It," Knight Foundation, www.knightfoundation.org, December 7, 2017.
5. Jennifer Miller, "Have We Hit Peak Podcast?" *New York Times*, July 18, 2019.
6. Jim Epstein, "Why Government Funding Hurts PBS and NPR," reason.com, February 17, 2017.
7. David Boaz, "Why PBS is a Public Menace," New York Post, June 2, 2011.
8. Clark, "Public Broadcasting," *CQ Researcher*: 4.
9. Epstein, "Why Government Funding Hurts PBS and NPR," reason.com.
10. "Knight Foundation Reports Explore Evolving Role of Public Media," http:// philanthrophynewsdigest.org, December 12, 2017.
11. Knight Foundation, "Public Media at 50: Looking to the Future," www.knight foundation.org, December 7, 2017.
12. Melody Kramer and Betsy O'Donovan, "F is for Future: How to Think About Public Media's Next 50 Years," Knight Foundation, www.knightfoundatio n.org, December 7, 2017.
13. Sue Gardner, "Public Broadcasting: Its Past and Future," Knight Foundation, December 7, 2017, www.knightfoundation.org.
14. Daniel Guerra, "U.S. repeals ban on broadcasting Voice of America, other government-funded news for American audiences," Knight Center for Journalism in the Americas, July 17, 2013, https://knightcenter.utexas.edu/blog/ 00-14160-us-repeals-ban-broadcasting-voice-america-other-government-fun ded-news-american-audien.
15. Trevor Burrus, "International Public Broadcasting Can Come Home, But Do We Need It at All?" *Daily Caller*, July 17, 2013.
16. Ragusea, "Topple the Towers: Why Public Radio and Television Stations Should Radically Reorient Toward Digital-First Local News, and How They Could Do It," Knight Foundation.
17. McLoughlin and Gomez, "The Corporation for Public Broadcasting: Federal Funding and Issues," Congressional Research Service, p. 8.

18. Elizabeth Grieco, "U.S. newsroom employment has dropped by a quarter since 2008, with greatest decline at newspapers," Pew Research Center, July 9, 2019, https://www.pewresearch.org/fact-tank/2019/07/09/u-s-newsroom-employment-has-dropped-by-a-quarter-since-2008/.

19. Trevor Burrus, "Why NPR and PBS Should Stop Taking Government Money," *Daily Beast*, April 2, 2017.

20. Gonzalez, "Is There Any Justification for Continuing to Ask Taxpayers to Fund NPR and PBS?" Knight Foundation.

21. Husock, "Public broadcasting shouldn't get a handout from taxpayers anymore," *Washington Post*.

22. Howard Husock, "Public broadcasting can survive, and even improve, without federal subsidies," *The Hill*, June 8, 2017.

23. Howard Husock, "Public media must reimagine itself for a new era—or give up 'reason to exist,' " *Current*, December 7, 2018, www.current.org.

24. Howard Husock, "To Combat the 'Rigging' Charge, National Public Radio Should Be More…National," *National Review* (November 1, 2016).

25. Howard Husock, "A New Role for Public Broadcasting?" *National Affairs* (Spring 2015): 103.

26. Ibid.: 108.

27. Husock, "Public media must reimagine itself for a new era—or give up 'reason to exist,'" *Current*.

28. Walker, "With Friends Like These: Why Community Radio Does Not Need the Corporation for Public Broadcasting," Cato Institute.

29. Walker, *Rebels on the Air: An Alternative History of Radio in America*, p. 147.

Printed by Books on Demand, Germany